Real
Your
Power

7-STEPS TO SORT YOUR SELF OUT

Alan Lucas

realiseyourpower.com

Beak Street

First published in 2023 by Beak Street Publishing

Copyright © Alan Lucas, 2023

ISBN 978-1-915036-95-7
Also available as an ebook
ISBN 978-1-915036-96-4

Design and illustrations by User Design,
    Illustration and Typesetting
Cover by Karen Lilje
Printed and bound in Suffolk by Clays,
    Ltd, Elcograf S.p.A.

MIX
Paper from
responsible sources
FSC® C018072

For more information visit realiseyourpower.com

Disclaimer

The information in this book is designed to provide ideas on how to think differently about life. Any opinions and suggestions by the author are merely that, and the author and publisher offer no warranties or guarantees for any of the content or how it is applied. You are responsible for your own choices, actions and results.

Although the author and publisher have made every effort to ensure all information in this book was correct at the time of going to press, the author and publisher do not assume and hereby disclaim any liability to any party for any loss, damage or disruption caused by errors or omissions, whether such errors or omissions result from negligence, accident or any other cause.

None of the material in this book is meant to be used, nor should it be used, to diagnose or treat any medical condition. The book is not intended as a substitute for the medical advice of doctors and the reader should consult their medical practitioner for advice in relation to any suspected medical condition.

About Alan Lucas

Alan Lucas was born and raised in Belfast during the troubles and wondered from a young age why people would kill others just because they had developed different beliefs.

After university he worked as a ski teacher in the United States, New Zealand, Australia and Europe, followed by a 12-year marketing career at global sportswear brands Nike and Adidas.

He has founded various businesses and trained across a range of psychology, psychotherapy and coaching disciplines to create the highly effective 7-Step – Sort Your Self Out System®.

As an author, entrepreneur and motivational speaker, Alan is passionate about self-improvement and helping people have more fun and fulfilling lives.

He is the author of *You Don't Need Therapy*®, and creator of the Less Ego® brand, which donates profits to the SYSO Foundation, providing free personal development resources to young people to help them make the most of their lives.

Alan speaks in schools and colleges for free. To contact Alan or to support the SYSO Foundation please visit realiseyourpower.com or email info@realiseyourpower.com

If you want things to change,
you have to change.

Contents

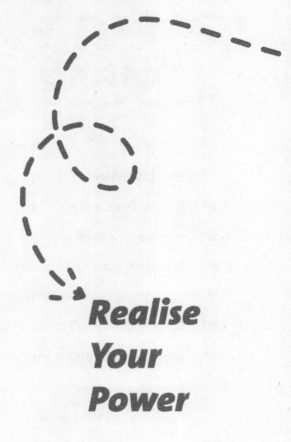

Realise
Your
Power

The SYSO System

'How much power do you believe you have to make your life better?' I asked.

'None,' she said. 'None at all. I have no money. I live in a s**t town, my family don't understand me and I hate my colleagues and my job. People are mean, I'm bored and I just want to get away.'

'Get away where?' I asked.

'Anywhere that makes me happy,' she replied.

Emily was 17. She felt lost and miserable. I worked with lots of individuals like her. People who felt disempowered and disillusioned, and who looked at their life and talked to themselves in ways that were guaranteed to make them feel helpless. Emily wasn't happy and believed she had very little power to change that. She was complaining about her problems and wishing things could be different.

Emily believed that 'getting away' was her answer, but until she worked on her own self-improvement she wouldn't be able to 'get away' from how she looked at life.

I worked with Emily to help her see things differently. She quickly stopped waiting and wishing, and instead started creating the life she wanted. She got in the driving seat. Her world changed, because she changed. She realised she had the power within to feel better about her life and to make more of her experience, no matter what the current situation. She decided to take responsibility for her life and wake up to the immensity of her potential and the limitless opportunities life provides. Not only did her life become more fulfilling, but in her becoming more, those around her benefitted. Growing was better for Emily and better for everyone.

She did 'get away'. She travelled far and wide, but not because she was trying to escape herself. She fell in love with herself. It didn't matter where she went, she enjoyed her own company and knew she was in charge of the life she was creating. She shone.

Life is full of people who have endured all kinds of unimaginable pain and suffering, yet somehow they have been able to move forward and create a better life for themselves, full of joy and happiness. They turned their pain to power and chose to make their life better.

They realised their own power to decide, to choose, to grow and to change, and no matter what happened in their outside world, they were able to control how they felt on the inside.

Changing your life can happen quickly when you commit to improving yourself. It's not complicated, you just need to know what to do, and then do it. If you follow the principles of the 7-Step Sort Your Self Out (SYSO) System, you'll change how you think, which will change how you feel, which will change what you do, all as quickly as you choose.

This book reveals the same seven steps I worked through with Emily and many others.

☞ *Realising your power means becoming aware of the power you have and then activating yourself to use it: awareness and action. The 7-Step Sort Your Self Out (SYSO) System is a concise and practical system to guide you in doing that. The system cuts through the deep forest of existing self-improvement material and distils into a universal solution seven principles that can be applied wherever you are on your journey.*

If you want to make changes to your life, read the book, and do what it says. The system is simple. Seven chapters. Seven Steps. By following the Steps, you will change the filter through which you experience life, and by changing the filter, everything will look different. You will have a new perspective, clarity of purpose and gratitude for the gift of life. Each step amplifies the others, and you can revisit any step at any time to really engrain your learning.

The system is straightforward and this book is filled with exercises so you can DO the changing, rather than just read about it. The exercises are simple and mostly quick to do, requiring little more than a pen and paper or making notes on your phone or computer. Practise these exercises as often as you like.

To have an excellent life, like training to be excellent at anything, involves regular practice and developing helpful habits. Making an outstanding life isn't a single event; it is an ongoing journey of growth and development.

Thank your previous self for getting you to this point and for all the lessons, but now it's time to upgrade. No more settling, much more creating. Creating the person you can be and the life you want. Commit to a better life. Wake up to the immensity of your potential.

It's up to you.

Start now.

Realise Your Power.

STEP 1

Become More Aware

Awareness is the greatest agent for change.

Eckhart Tolle

There are approximately 7.7 billion people on this planet today, and each year new arrivals and fewer departures bring a net addition of around 80 million. However, those of us currently living represent only about 7% of the total number of humans who have ever lived. Since modern *Homo sapiens* first walked the earth around 50,000 years ago, more than 108 billion members of our species have existed. Altogether, dead and alive, that is a lot of human life!

The actual numbers can be hard to put in perspective at that scale. Think of the largest number of people you have ever seen together at any time, either in person at an event, in photographs or even in film. Massive music festivals like Glastonbury or Coachella host around 200,000 and 120,000 people respectively, and occasionally there are huge, one-off religious festivals or celebrations that involve hundreds of thousands or even a few million people. But the numbers still represent only a tiny fraction of the number of people alive right now, today, on Earth, and an even tinier fraction of all the human beings who have ever lived.

You are unique

The number of human beings that have been created is remarkable, but even more so is the fact that every single one, wherever and whenever they have lived, is a different *expression* of life. So, 108 billion different versions of people have been produced so far in the story of humanity, and no two are the same. It's a fact; you are truly unique and special among the billions. You are not one in a million.

 You are one in 108 billion! Congratulations!

Everything we can see of the human body is unique, and everything we cannot see – our brains, our hearts, our blood cells, our gut – everything inside us is also a bespoke unique-to-us design. We are evolving from the same ingredients, but are different expressions of humanness.

As our *thoughts and emotions* are created by our bodies, it makes sense that how we think and how we feel will also be different from every other human being. You are supposed to be different to everyone else. So, first things first: as you start working through the SYSO System, take a few moments to really appreciate the amazingness of your bespoke, one-off design. Really appreciate the remarkable one-in-all-the-lifetimes creation that you are.

A human being is a single being. Unique and unrepeatable.

Eileen Caddy

EXERCISE 1
Appreciate Your Uniqueness

Find somewhere quiet and without distraction. Be still and breathe deeply and slowly – in through your nose and out through your mouth.

Each breath in is bringing new oxygen to energise every cell in your body, and each breath out is getting rid of waste in the form of carbon dioxide. Now imagine all the negative thoughts and toxins leaving your body as waste with each exhalation.

Each day you will take around 23,000 breaths and your heart will beat about 100,000 times, all without requiring you to consciously do anything. Appreciate the beautiful gifts of your breathing and heart beating.

Think about your blood flowing around your vessels and how incredible this system is. Every part of your body is working together to make you unique.

Become more aware of the uniqueness of your ears, your eyes, your fingerprints, your tongue, your skin. You were designed to be unique. You were designed to be special.

You're an amazing creation. Breathe deeply and appreciate yourself. Carry on taking deep breaths in and long, slow, relaxing breaths out until you are ready to finish.

All life is unique

In all our unique forms, as humans, we are *not alone in living* on this planet. We share Earth with an estimated 8.7 million other species of life, all of which are also individually different by design. Difference *is* life.

Humans are relative newcomers. We have only lived for a fraction of the time this planet has existed, and the history of all animals that have been recorded from fossils is only about 15% of the recorded history of all life on Earth. There is a lot more to life than just us.

If we look beyond our little planet, even though there is much still being discovered, we know that all planets and all solar systems are different in each galaxy, and there are billions of galaxies in our universe. Nothing is the same as anything else. Everything is different. Everything is unique.

We should question any thoughts about humans somehow being superior to other forms of life. What if everything was *different, but completely equal* and just as valuable as any other part of the whole system of life? We are all part of the universe. As humans, we tend to think of ourselves as individual and separate and it may well be that this delusion of separateness and sense of hierarchy is at the heart of many of our emotional problems. We will explore this further throughout the book and especially in Step 6 when we look at the interconnectedness of all life.

☞ *The bottom line is that nature is difference. Life and nature are diversity. It was designed to be that way and we should celebrate this diversity.*

To be beautiful means to be yourself. When you are born a lotus flower, be a beautiful lotus flower, don't try to be a magnolia flower.

Thich Nhat Hanh

EXERCISE 2
Build Your Sensory Awareness

Take a few moments to think about the uniqueness that is everything in nature, then focus specifically on each of your senses in turn.

Think about your sight. Look around, see what you can see, the colours, shades, textures, any movement. There is always more to see. Try and look for something new in the same situation.

Think about your hearing and all the sounds you are aware of and how the sound is changing and moving. Be aware of the pitch, the tempo, the loudness, the duration, the source of the soundwaves and how they are reaching you. Think about how these sounds make your feel.

Think about tastes and how you can determine different flavours. Think about the textures of food and how easy it is to chew.

Think about smell. Humans detect smells by inhaling air that contains odour molecules, which then bind to receptors inside the nose, relaying messages to the brain.

Think about your sense of touch and the feelings you have.
Think about how you experience touch. Touch your face,
your fingernails, the different texture in your knuckles,
your palms and the back of your hand. Touch your hair,
your eyelashes and your clothes. Feel the differences.

Now reflect on this exercise and the ability you have
to process life through your senses.

You are an incredible force of nature. Start noticing it more.
Notice your place in the system of nature. Notice leaves,
flowers, bees, birds, clouds, trees, grass, soil. The more you
look at nature the more you will see and appreciate its
astonishing design and diversity and the more you will
appreciate being a part of life.

If you aren't inspired, look again.

Paul Smith

Different, but equal

Become more aware of being different but also know that everyone is equal. *Different, but equal.* Rather than comparing yourself to others, focus on being the best version of your unique self and not on what other people are doing or how they are living; we all have our own unique set of qualities, thoughts, beliefs, emotions and values.

It's only when we start comparing components of one person to components of another that we start thinking of one person being 'better' than another. It's healthy to compete, but winning in one area doesn't mean winning overall. Nobody can be the 'most' in every area as we all have different capabilities and capacities. The best is only really important in terms of the 'best you', as there will always be some part or you measured against someone else that will be 'better' or 'worse'. What if, instead, we focused more on human *qualities* like kindness, compassion and gratitude? Our capacity in these areas, which are non-physical, is unlimited.

When we are acutely tuned into our individuality and uniqueness we are already more aware of life. It is in becoming more aware of ourselves, of others and of our environment that we can start to really grow as humans and to have the best life possible.

> *Let's look for the things to be grateful for, and celebrate our differences – for wouldn't the world be rather boring if we were all the same?*

Richard Branson

Developing self-awareness

Awareness of our physical uniqueness is only the starting point. It is awareness of who we are as a person, our *invisible* forces and how we behave that is at the core of all personal development and the power we have as human beings. Without self-awareness, our thoughts, feelings and behaviour are controlled by our unconscious beliefs, instincts, habits and values, which we're unlikely to have ever questioned (see Step 2). If our quality of life is essentially about how we feel, then we need to have awareness about how and why we are feeling something if we want to take charge and change it (see Step 3).

Realise Your Power

If you want to be happier, you first need to be aware of how you are being, thinking and feeling, and to take responsibility for this. It is actually more accurate and helpful to think about *doing* happiness rather than *being* happy, as feelings are things we *do*. We are really humans *doing* rather than humans *being*, and when we understand this, we open the door to taking responsibility for – and realising we have the choice about – the feelings we *do*.

EXERCISE 3

Become Aware of Emotional Triggers

Think of a time recently when you were angry or frustrated. Now think of what happened just before that moment.

You didn't just get angry; some thought patterns kicked in and you 'did' a process in your brain. (More of what happens with these processes in Steps 2 *and* 3 *.)*

Remember what triggered your anger thoughts. How did those thoughts make you feel? How long did it last?

Draw a line across a blank sheet of paper representing the path of your anger from before the trigger to after the feeling had passed. Were you content and calm and then gradually you became angry? Or did you suddenly spike up and change

*your feelings immediately? Mark this path on your paper
and write down the length of time these feelings lasted.*

*Then think about what happened to change your feelings
over the course of your graph. Was there a distraction?
Did you change your thoughts or perspective? Did you
feel like your anger 'burnt out' or disappeared naturally?
Did something external change your thoughts and feelings?*

*Your answers and the 'anger timeline' you have just drawn,
don't have to be precise; this is just an exercise to help you
start tuning in to how you are feeling and why.*

*Becoming more aware of ourselves, what we are feeling
and why, allows us to take charge of processing and
managing the feelings we want.*

It all starts with awareness.

We can't control that which is outside ourselves, but through
self-awareness we can control our *responses* and therefore
have a choice over how we feel. This is the key to *doing*
happy.

Identify your own bad habits

The first step of change is to become more aware of our
own unhelpful habits. If you want to give up a habit that

isn't serving you well, the more awareness you have about what motivates you, how you are thinking and the emotions you're feeling, the more you'll be able to change your behaviour and create a higher quality of life. Your behaviour is really just *patterns of* thinking, habits and emotions. Change can actually happen instantly when you become more aware and take the right actions to change patterns that aren't helping you lead the life you want.

 Self-awareness is the starting platform from which to learn how to change.

The sooner we can become more aware, the better, or it will only be when we face a big problem in life that we'll be forced to face ourselves truly.

Often we *react* to our emotions and feelings, but if we are aware of them and not at the mercy of them, we can take charge. Build awareness of yourself and take charge of growing and becoming more, and your outer world will change.

You have responsibility

Think of a time when you felt really angry because of something someone said to you. What did they say?

Were you really offended? Only you know exactly how you reacted then or in other situations like this, but as you develop your awareness, you will start reacting differently and feeling differently. First, you'll appreciate that other people's words and actions are not yours, unless you choose to take them on board. You can't control how others behave and what they say, but you can control your reaction to them and it's your choice of reaction that will determine your feelings. Can someone hurt you by something they say? Only if you allow them to.

Imagine someone approaches you who you think is very drunk and aggressive. You've seen them shout angrily and aggressively at others and now they approach you, asking loudly if you're colour blind because who else would wear shoes like yours? Are you going to allow what they say to affect what you feel about your choice of shoes? What if you later found out they had a serious illness that made them wildly irrational and verbally aggressive? Would you think differently about the interaction? The reality is we don't ever really know what's going on in other people's heads and so we shouldn't give up our power to something outside of ourselves, which we don't likely understand anyway.

The key is to understand or be aware of what is happening and why, and then *take charge of the meaning you attach* to this and choose your response. You'll learn much more about this and exercises to practise throughout the book, especially in Steps 2 and 3. If you follow the SYSO System, you'll be the boss of your own life experience, not at the mercy of things that happen *to* you.

Clarity precedes success

If you're not achieving your goals in life the first question to ask is, are you clear on what your goals are, and why? Without absolute *clarity* about what you want to achieve, you're not going to get there. It all starts with *awareness* and removing the bullshit blocks we have accumulated. Imagine I'm not happy in my friendships or with my finances or fitness (or all of these). Without knowing why, and without knowing clearly what I really want, I'll find myself stuck and probably very frustrated.

> *Our greatness lies not so much in being able to remake the world as being able to remake ourselves.*

Mahatma Gandhi

You have everything you need within you, right here, right now, to make the changes you need in your life.

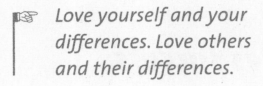

Love yourself and your differences. Love others and their differences.

It's miraculous that you, or any of us, even exist.

Self-awareness is your superpower

By now, it should be loud and clear: the first foundation and step of the SYSO System is to become more *aware*. Become more aware of yourself, of your power, of others and of your environment. When you become more aware and notice more, you appreciate how incredible life really is.

So, all this sounds good in theory but how do you actually become more aware? You simply decide to! You choose to, and then you take action, and this book has the tools to help you take this action. The more aware you become, the more you will discover how much there is to be aware of! Your life will be richer and you will be able to make changes to things you probably never realised were holding you back.

Decide now and start practising. Self-awareness allows you to appreciate your individuality (and everyone else's). It is a quest to always keep building your awareness 'muscles', to be conscious of the physical, but also of the invisible

forces in you. *Self-awareness* allows you to make changes
to the thoughts, beliefs and interpretations in your mind,
which affect your emotions and experience of life.

EXERCISE 4

Observe Your Thoughts

Sit comfortably with your feet flat on the floor and just breathe deeply and relax. Close your eyes.

As you relax, imagine all the stresses draining away from your body and appreciate each breath bringing in new, fresh energy. Focus on the feeling of your chest moving and each exhale releasing tension.

When you feel completely relaxed, think about what thoughts you're having. Observe them as if they are passing in front of you and then dissolving as they float on by.

They are just thoughts. You are not your thoughts. You are the awareness of them.

If you get distracted, keep coming back to your breath.

You can do this at any time and in any place. As you practise, you will be building your awareness muscle.

Until you are aware in the moment of your thoughts, emotions, language and behaviours, you will have difficulty making significant changes in your life.

☞ *As you build your self-awareness, you'll realise you are in control, and you can choose how you want to think and feel. You'll empower yourself.*

We can't control a lot of what happens to us in life, but we can always control our response.

Every time you are tempted to react in the same old way, ask if you want to be a prisoner of the past or a pioneer of the future.

Deepak Chopra

What's your personality type?

One useful tool in any self-awareness work to is to have a simple way you can think about different personality or behaviour types. As we know, we are all unique, and therefore technically there are more than 7 billion personality types, but it can be helpful to have a simple framework you can use to quickly assess personalities generally, even if the concept of personality types is a little contradictory. I like simple, clear and easy to use frameworks, and in my experience for accurateness and *simplicity* a test called DISC is good.

The DISC tool is a behaviour assessment based on the theory of psychologist, William Marston, and which centres on four different personality types. These can broadly be classified as Dominance, Influence, Steadiness and Conscientiousness. The exercise involves a series of questions and four answer options, which you place in priority according to how you believe the answers best describe you. The collective answers you give come together to rate you against four different measures. However, you can get a glimpse into these personality classifications by asking two simple questions, which will help you gain a good idea of your own, or someone else's, behaviour profile at a very basic, but useful, level. It's also good to remember that we may express a different type of personality in different environments, so context is important.

EXERCISE 5
What's Your Personality Type?

Start with a blank sheet of paper and a pen and ask yourself the following two questions:

Q1

Do you consider yourself more extroverted or introverted?

Draw a vertical line in the centre of your page. At the top end of the line write 'extroverted'. At the bottom end of the line write 'introverted'. Then, using your best intuitive estimate, think where you would place yourself on this line/ axis in terms of whether you consider yourself more extrovert or introvert.

Q2

When doing tasks with others, are you more focused on the people and their feelings or on getting the task done?

Now draw a horizontal line across the middle of the vertical line you have made, and on this line, write 'task' on the left end and 'people' on the right. On this horizontal line/ axis, think about whether you prioritise people and their feelings or getting the task done, and then position yourself on that axis. There's no need to try and be 'exact' and there is no correct answer.

You will now have two lines crossing each other in the centre and four quadrants, and the answers you have given to these two questions above will determine in which quadrant your personality is most likely to fit.

If you positioned yourself in the top left quadrant, you will most likely be someone whose behaviour is more outgoing, who is focused primarily on getting the task done. If you see yourself as sitting in the top right quadrant, you will most likely be outgoing, but your focus will be primarily on people.

In the bottom right, the priority is people and you consider yourself more reserved or introverted. In the bottom left quadrant, you're introverted but focused on the task and getting results.

The four quadrants are not definitive and exact, and the tool is more about priorities and variations in degree, so this is definitely not about labelling or rigidly classifying behaviour. Rather, it is just one very simple tool that can be helpful in creating greater awareness of different personalities.

The benefit is to invite thinking about how you and others will behave in certain situations. Aiming to understand others, rather than judging their behaviour, will change your relationships dramatically, although the starting point is always understanding ourselves first, and there are many ways to practise this.

Write to bring clarity

To help get *focus and clarity* about who we are and why we act and behave in a certain way, writing stuff down is an incredibly powerful practice and it's smart to make a habit of doing this. It doesn't require you to be endlessly writing and it can be in whichever format is easiest; pen and paper or on your phone or electronic device. The act of writing and taking notes makes the invisible thoughts visible and helps direct your mind (see more in Step 2).

EXERCISE 6
Use Writing to Focus

The purpose of this exercise is to help focus your thoughts and to become more aware of how you are 'doing' your life. Of course, you can write whatever is important to how you think and feel and the goals you have. Start making notes, not writing long sentences. This is just to bring some focus to your thoughts, feelings, behaviour and actions.

Here are some examples of the things you can write:

- *Journal your feelings. Perhaps note the time, the place, what you are feeling and why you believe you are feeling this way. Find a simple way of noting this that works for you.*

- *Create a list of qualities you value most in human behaviour.*

- *Write a list of what is important to you and the life you want.*

- *Start writing specific goals for your future.*

- *Write down the number of times you laughed and smiled in a day.*

- *Make a list of things you are grateful for.*

- *Write a list of the most important people in your life and why.*

- *Write a letter to yourself, as if you were at the very end of your life. What have you learnt about yourself and life and what would you do differently.*

These are just some examples of areas in which you can start making notes, but the key is to start! Once you begin, you will feel more focused and by writing these thoughts down, you are taking charge in the process of building your self-awareness.

How do you talk to yourself?

Do you pay much attention to how you talk to yourself? Self-talk, as we shall cover in Step 2, is a critical component of how you think about who you are and how you're directing yourself in life. You might never actually have thought about it much, but we tend to talk a lot to ourselves in our heads. Being aware of how we are talking to ourselves and whether this is helpful or not can enable us to then build a more empowering, positive and fun dialogue with ourselves.

Tune into the language you and others use. Language makes a huge difference to how we feel. Use more emphatic, positive, enthusiastic, *empowering language* and your life will change through that alone. Not only will upbeat language make you feel better, but your biochemistry changes when you use more uplifting words.

If you have read this chapter, Step 1 of the SYSO System, and practised the exercises, you'll already be building your awareness muscles and life will be becoming different. Regularly remind yourself that you are unique and special, that everyone is unique and special and we are all equal and essential parts of life. You are unique, you are loved, you are enough, and *all* you need is within you.

As a human you are 'doing' living, you are 'doing' behaviour. When you understand this and are aware of what you're doing and why, you can take responsibility for your life and start effecting changes more easily.

As you build your awareness muscles, you will also become more aware of others and the world around you. Realising that there is so much we don't know makes us less rigidly opinionated and opens our hearts and minds, allowing us to feel grateful and curious and keep perspective. We become more understanding of others and less judgemental; showing compassion is our core human nature.

Smile, appreciate all the beauty and relax into knowing we can't know everything in this lifetime. Enjoy the journey and your new expanded filter for your experience of being alive.

Everything in the universe is within you.

Rumi

STEP 2
Manage
Your
Mind

You either control your mind
or it controls you.

Napoleon Hill

When you actively decide to manage your mind and be in control of how you think, rather than just reacting to the thoughts you have, you'll transform how you feel and what you do. It really is that straightforward. How you think affects what you feel, and how you feel affects what you do, and what you feel and do is your life!

We're mostly taught *what* to think and sometimes *why* to think it, but there isn't much focus on the *how* of thinking. *How to think more effectively* and deliberately, to make the most of your life.

When you work on how you think, you'll grow and *become more* as a person, which, as opposed to *getting more*, is the key to feeling fulfilled in life. Become the manager of your mind, rather than a casual labourer to it.

Train your brain

There's often an assumption that thinking is just something you do automatically because of the brain you were born with, and that you can't, or don't need to, train your brain to think in a better way. Most people are just living by reacting to, rather than being the manager of their thoughts. These thoughts are in control of us, not the other way around, but we can train ourselves to think more effectively for the life we want, and it all starts with awareness. Become more aware of what thinking is, and take control of the patterns that are created in your brain, and you'll be in the driving seat of your life and your journey.

You'll also become more understanding of how others are thinking, and so become more understanding of their behaviour, which leads to more tolerance, and a greater ability to have influence and enjoy better relationships in all areas of your life.

Thinking is the programming or software creator of your brain, which determines what you feel and do. The software runs us, but other than the basic in-built human survival and operating programmes which we all have, most of the rest of our software has been developed without our being aware it is even software. We just think it's the way we're made, but our behaviour is not who we are at our core; it is the result of the programming we have taken on and the thinking patterns of this programming.

Mind health

We understand about training our bodies for health, but we seldom talk about training or programming our minds for health. Yet mind health will determine the quality of our life.

Our brain is a processor and it runs processes. We need to work on the processes and how we are 'doing' them because when we change these, we change our feelings and we change our life.

We have the capability to recondition our thinking to create new processes, or patterns, which will change the 'wiring' and the chemical mix of our brains. We can upgrade our software to upgrade our life.

Most people aren't aware of their thinking processes or believe it's just 'not that easy' to make changes to their thinking. People who are struggling to change some behaviour often say things like 'I just can't help it'. Taking 100% responsibility for what we do and how we feel is the foundation of creating the life we want. We can't control things outside ourselves, but we can control our inner world and we can take responsibility for how we think and how we feel. We have the power over our thinking so all that we have to do is use this power.

The brain is designed to work for us, and it's our *unconscious* (we'll learn more about this later) that runs most of our behaviour like an autopilot. We just need to give *directions* and tell the brain to do the processes that will cause the thoughts, feelings and behaviour we want. These forces for thinking, feeling and behaving are all inside us. Everything we need is within us right here, right now.

> *I don't fix problems. I fix my thinking. Then problems fix themselves.*

Louise L. Hay

Taking charge

When we take charge of our thinking, we can train our minds to take action that will get the results we want in any area of our life. What we don't change, we are actively choosing not to. We need to train our brains to focus on the solutions and not waste time overanalysing the problems. Most people know how to change but perhaps don't have a strong enough reason for wanting to make the change, or they have an emotional block or resistance to change, which is getting in their way. We will learn in this Step how to deal with these invisible blocks to taking action and we'll practice some exercises to train our minds for successful change, in whatever area of our life we choose.

You don't need a PhD in psychology to have sufficient understanding of the brain's basic workings to maximise its effectiveness. Study and inquire as much as you want, of course, but in the meantime the SYSO System is about focusing on the life you are going to create. The SYSO System is about very practical psychology. So, start right now. Commit to training and managing your mind for success.

Your brain didn't come with manual

Don't beat yourself up if your current *programming* isn't working for you; we need to know how to use the amazing brain we have, but it didn't come with an instruction manual and we're not usually taught formally at school about brain management and how to think. We may have taken on programming that was perhaps helpful for a different time or from people around us rather than actively taking charge and programming ourselves for the life we want. Opinions and other people's beliefs are pushed upon us by the media, family and our peer groups, but do we stop and ask where these opinions have come from and why they are believed?

☞ *You can either be unaware and programmed by the messages around you, or you can take charge and programme yourself for the life you want. Which would you prefer?*

Our education system has traditionally put a lot of emphasis on generalised and conventional tests to measure people's 'Intelligence Quotient' (IQ) but these tests only measure one dimension of something that has been defined as intelligence. There are many types of intelligence in human life and in nature, and everyone is equally intelligent when we broaden the definition to allow for different capabilities and capacities. We know every brain – and the processes within each – is unique, yet society is increasingly ascribing labels to classify people if they seem different to those considered 'normal'.

We know that we're all different and different in different ways (Step 1), and we should do more to harness people's uniqueness, rather than label individuals, which often happens in a negative way.

Understand and celebrate them. We are all weaker and stronger in some areas of our learning than others because we are all different. We are also just running processes and *processes can be changed.*

Neuroplasticity

Scientists used to believe that your brain can't change much and that you were born with a biologically pre-determined brain. More recent research, however, shows that the brain can and does change throughout life, not just in ways of thinking but physically too. This process is called neuroplasticity, as we change in response to our behaviour, environment and thinking. We can grow more brain cells, and create more and better connections between cells.

The brain is a tool to work for us. It just needs our management and direction. Its primary objective is to help us process information in order to stay alive and be energy-efficient in doing so. It has a negativity bias built-in to help with survival and this evolved through what was a dangerous world for our ancestors; it is constantly looking out for threats and what is wrong. It isn't naturally programmed to look for what is right; what's right isn't a danger, so the brain is acutely sensitive to bad experiences, because it wants to protect us. This may explain why we tend to hang onto bad experiences for so long.

When we have good experiences, most of us are not good at installing these and learning from them. We need to wire ourselves proactively to feel better faster. We need to notice what's right more often rather than being hunters of faults.

> *Your mind is programmable. If you're not programming your mind, someone else will program it for you.*

Jeremy Hammond

Programming

Think of two newborn babies. All they essentially want to do is feed, sleep, pass their waste, keep warm, move, and be held, and if they don't get these things they become agitated and cry. This is the basic in-built programming of being human, or the functioning and survival programme we all have from birth. As they grow, each child will develop a different set of things they *believe* and *value* in their world. They'll become wired differently based on their experiences, their environment, their parents and their peer group.

For most people as they develop, the programming happens without them being aware it's even programming, but it happens anyway.

☞ *To become a manager of our mind, first we need to become more aware that we are in control of our programming. Then we need to guard our minds from unhelpful opinions and beliefs that attempt to programme us without permission.*

Think of your brain like it's your beautiful, unique house that you built, full of amazing detail and decor. Say you had a party and some people wanted to come in and make trouble, or change the atmosphere or start being destructive. Would you let anyone into your house, at any time, to do whatever they wanted to do? Of course you wouldn't. You would stand guard and decide who came into your home. In the same way, we should stand guard at the door of our mind. We all have lots of thoughts, and the key is to channel the effective ones and let the others go. So, decide now, as you read this, that you are going to take control of your mind and your brain programming. You are going to manage and direct your brain because now you know you can.

EXERCISE 7
Decide to Be in Charge of Your Mind

Find a place where you won't be disturbed.

Decide now that you are going to be in charge. You know your brain is designed to work for you. You are going to give your brain directions.

Write down the following phrase which you are going to make the primary programming incantation for your mind.

- *MY brain works FOR me.*

- *I control MY brain and direct it to SERVE me, I manage MY brain to get the results I want.*

- *I do not negotiate with my brain.*

Repeat this multiple times, stick it on a Post-it note above your desk or make it a screensaver, wherever you need to put it as a reminder that you are in charge and you are going to train your brain for the life you want.

Managing your mind starts with giving clear direction. Don't negotiate with your brain, it is a tool that works for you.

Become an observer of your thoughts

If you have a brain there will be thoughts. Neuroscientists don't really know where thoughts actually come from, but it is estimated that we have about 60,000 to 80,000 thoughts every day and most of them are the same thoughts we had yesterday! The key to effective mind management is to filter and channel thoughts and create an environment for empowering and useful new thoughts to develop.

When we're aware, we can decide to use the thoughts that are helpful for our clear goals and just let the thoughts that aren't relevant or helpful pass by or dissolve. There is so much going on in our thoughts that unless we become great at *filtering* and *focusing*, our head will be full of chatter and become overwhelmed.

Celebrate your capacity to create thoughts and to be able to just observe them. Don't feel bad or guilty if you have thoughts that you wish you didn't have; everyone has these, they're just thoughts. Thoughts don't mean anything; they're not who you are, they come and go all the time. When you practise observing your thoughts from a distance, you're watching them and therefore they can't be you.

Give your brain focus or targets for your thoughts. Start by asking yourself what life you want and describe it as clearly as you can. People often describe what they don't want, but the key is to have clarity about what you do want otherwise your brain will be confused. If you went to the supermarket and someone asked you not to get milk, oranges and bread, is that going to help you to buy what you do need? The unconscious mind doesn't understand negatives and it won't be helpful to tell it what you don't want. Clarity is essential and you must tell your unconscious mind what you want.

How your brain works

Your brain, as I have already said, is a processor, constantly processing. It's the most complex part of our bodies, weighing on average around 1.5 kg in an adult, and it is made mostly of water and fat. It's the brain cells and the connections between these cells that really make the brain work or *do* the thinking.

Neuroscientists generally agree the brain is composed of two types of cells, neurons and neuroglia cells, and it's neurons that create our thinking and programming. We have lots of them. It is estimated there are over 100 billion, but even neuroscientists don't know for certain, and like each of us, every neuron is different and unique. Like a muscle in our body, using our brain is the key to realising its potential, but only if we're using it effectively.

When a baby is born it starts to create programmes in its mind such as 'If I cry, I get food', or 'If I touch that heater, it feels uncomfortable', or any number of early experiences as it tries to survive and be loved. This processing of information, filtered by learning, is the basis of how we develop our behaviour and what we believe and value. We start to learn about consequences and trade-offs and choices. These experiences cause the *building of connections* in the brain which is programming being installed. Although it is in the early years that we embed many programmes that stay with us for life, we can at any time throughout our life re-programme our connections once we become aware and know what to do. So, how does this programming or 'wiring' actually work and what can you do to install new programming?

Electricity and chemicals

It might sound like it's complicated, but brain science is really just about three things: electrical (brainwaves), architectural (brain structures) and chemical (neurochemicals) components, working together to create a state of mind.

Every time there is a thought, one of the brain's neurons fires an electrical pulse along an axon, which is like a 'wire'. At the end of an axon is a junction, which is a tiny gap, called a synapse and at the synapse the pulse causes the release of neurotransmitters. These are information-loaded chemicals, or chemical messengers, which then send signals to other neurons along lots of other axons. Electrical signals have to be changed to chemical signals to cross the gap, and these chemicals or neurotransmitters carry the information between the neurons by crossing the synapse. It is these chemicals or neurotransmitters that cause you to feel a certain way and which, in part, stimulate your energy flow.

Neurotransmitters are a blend of chemicals with different strengths and all are unique recipes or cocktails of chemicals that cross synapses to transmit impulses from a neuron to another cell. In other words, they're messengers carrying signals from one part of the brain to another (more on this in Step 3).

> *Everything should be made as simple as possible, but not simpler.*

Albert Einstein

In short, our thinking is *electricity and chemicals* working within our brain structure. We have the ability to manage and direct this electricity and these chemicals when we know how. This is the foundation to a successful and fulfilled life.

Your thought pathways

We know now that thoughts are the movement between neurons on pathways in the brain. A common analogy when learning about thought pathways is to imagine a path across a field of long grass. The more we go across the same path, the more beaten down it gets, turning the long grass to a flat, wider and more entrenched path, and so it becomes easier and quicker to cross. This is how we create pathways in our brains. The more we use the same thought path, the more we're programming and building thicker, superfast wires or neural pathways. Use the pathway and it will become beaten down, but stop using it and it will become overgrown again. This is the same whether our thoughts are helpful or unhelpful, positive or negative.

 Remember whatever we repeatedly think, we become.

So the question we should ask is, are the programmes we currently have serving us or limiting us?

Supercharge
your programming

Repeatedly thinking the same patterns creates wires
or pathways in our brain, but there are also things
that exponentially thicken these wires, make stronger
connections and create superfast, deeper wiring.
We can incorporate these tools to supercharge our
brain reprogramming.

When our thoughts have emotions attached, the pathways
become deeply entrenched and reinforced. This could
be through an emotionally intense experience, which is
positive, or it could be through a negative experience, which,
although we would like to forget it, keeps coming back to our
mind in a form of worry or regret.

When we move our body while 'doing' a thinking process,
we are also wiring deeper and faster and effectively waking
up our cells. It could be a hand in the air or fist pump saying,
for example, 'Come on!' or 'Yes!' when something great
happens. This engagement of your body and your mind
is a powerful way to enhance your wiring.

Programmed by our parents

Humans have the longest period of dependency of any animal and a lot of the programming we have is from our parents or primary carers because they're involved in a disproportionately large part of our lives. Parental intentions are usually good, and they do their best with the programming they have. But what if their thinking isn't that evolved or isn't as relevant for us in our lives at this time, as it was when they were at our stage of life?

Many of us have taken on our thinking patterns, beliefs and values from the programming our parents embedded in us as children. We then carry on through life without *examining* this until either we're forced to examine our own thinking by being confronted with a big life challenge, or we're moved through inspiration or our hunger to want to become more. For the majority of us, most of the programming we have assimilated from our parents has been helpful, but when we are aware of why and how we have the programming we do, we can change it, if we want to.

We can make sure our minds are working for us and the life we want, not our parents' lives or the life our parents want for us. We know that we can reprogramme ourselves and rewire our thinking, and we know how neurons fire up and send signals to other neurons. But how do you install this new programming most effectively for your life?

First, you need to decide on the life you want, so you have a clear direction for your thinking. Then you need to actively direct your brain to create the wiring, the neural pathways and patterns of connections to make this happen.

What are you focusing on?

In Step 5, we'll look at the importance of having a clear philosophy for the purpose of your life, and in the final 'Summary and Next Steps' section we'll look specifically at all the main areas of your life so you can design your own personal action plan.

The critical starting point is focus. *Where focus goes, energy flows*, and without focus an undirected mind will jump around all over the place, creating a more complicated and frustrating life as things aren't operating efficiently. The more we focus on something, the more other thoughts to support that focus will appear in our consciousness. This is mainly because of a little system in our brain called the reticular activating system (RAS) which, in very simple terms, is a bundle of nerves at our brainstem that filters out unnecessary information so the important stuff gets through. Your RAS works automatically, taking what you focus on and creating a filter for it, finding more to support what you are focusing on, without you noticing.

EXERCISE 8
What You Look for You See

Look around you for ten seconds and find everything you can see that is green. Look for green clothes, green leaves, green grass, green cars etc.

Now close your eyes and think about what you saw.

How much red did you see?

Almost certainly, you will not have seen much, if any red, because you simply were not looking for it. You just saw what you were looking for.

If you now do the same exercise but this time look for red, it's likely you will see lots of red.

Everything is out there, it just depends on what you are looking for. You see what you look for and your RAS is helping you to filter and focus.

If you are focusing on what you have, what you can control and the present, your RAS will be working to reinforce this positive empowering focus. If you're focusing on what's missing, what you can't control and the past, your RAS is going to find stuff to support that focus. In the same way, the RAS seeks information that validates your beliefs. It filters the world through the parameters you give it. If you think you're bad at maths then you probably will be. If you believe you are bad at public speaking then you probably will be. The RAS helps you see what you want to see and in doing so it influences your actions.

EXERCISE 9
What Are You Focusing On?

Ask yourself these three questions:

1. *Am I focusing on what I have or what is missing?*

2. *Am I focusing on what I can control or what is not in my control?*

3. *Am I focusing on the past, present or future?*

Keep this as a framework to ask yourself regularly to stay focused.

Make these questions a habitual reference point to keep your thinking in check. Focusing on what you have, what you can control and on being present and planning for the future is going to make your thinking more effective and give you a much more enjoyable experience of life.

Dealing with negative patterns

A lot of thoughts people have are to do with 'bad' things that have happened in the past, or worries or fears about something that might happen in the future. These repeated thoughts create pathways to not feeling great, and our RAS finds things to support these negative feelings and memories. When we say to ourselves 'this always happens to me', or 'life isn't fair', our brains are looking for things to support these beliefs. We often create patterns that repeat these bad memories over and over. We need to break these patterns and focus on the good stuff. It's impossible to process everything but when you have focus, your brain will operate more efficiently.

If we are focused, if we know where we are going and repeatedly make the same thoughts, we will create *powerful wiring* in our brains.

Linking emotion to fuel action

We can know what to do but still find it hard to change. Understanding alone is not enough to build superfast highways in our brains to create results. We need to link emotion to understanding because it's emotion that will be the fuel to determine action.

We can link an expectation of pain or pleasure to any thought and, together with understanding, this will be a powerful way to rewire our brains. If you want to change something, like eating less junk food, and link massive pain to the consequences of eating too much junk food, you will be likely to eat less. Think of the consequences if you carry on overeating; what will your life be like in one year, five years, ten years? What will it have cost you? What will you have missed out on? Is that going to make you feel good about your life? Now link massive pleasure to the future of eating healthier, by thinking of the *consequences*. What will your life be like if you feel full of energy and radiating health? What will that enable you to do? How will you look and feel? The deeper you visualise and feel the consequences of your behaviour, the more you will activate your emotions and the more you will want to choose the right path.

We have already discussed the power of movement to help supercharge your programming, and how you can embed successful action-activating thought patterns by incorporating your body as you are repeating the thoughts and linking emotion. Physically moving can be as simple as clenching your fist or raising your arms to the sky. The combination of having directed thoughts, linking emotion, and feeling it in your body as you move is the most powerful way to rewire yourself.

EXERCISE 10
Say Yes to Your Goals

Think of a clear goal and what you need to do to achieve that goal.

Now imagine you did the work and have already accomplished that goal.

Think of what it feels like and the consequences of achieving that. Think of how your life is different, how you have left the pain or dissatisfaction of where you were. Feel proud of the achievement and the steps you took to get there.

Now clench your fist as you imagine it done. When you clench your fist you are locking in the destination, and programming your mind for success.

As you repeatedly clench you fist, start chanting to yourself, simply saying over and over: 'yes', 'yes', 'yes', 'yes' ...

Get animated and drive your fist into the air. Move and get louder as you lock in that feeling of achieving your goal. You have done it. You are seeing, hearing and feeling your success.

Keep doing this and feel confident, proud, and alive as you imagine being in the moment of your achievement.

When you are ready, come back to the present.

You know you can and are going to make it happen. You are in control and you know in this state you can make anything happen.

You can change your emotional state at any time by changing your physiology and this is usually the best place to start. Physiology first. The body can give so much leverage to our thinking yet the body is often thought of as something separate from our brain, which is seen as the computer on our shoulders. However, everything is interconnected (Step 6) and you can radically change your life by tuning into how you move.

Using incantations

One of the most effective tools to put this focus, repetition, emotion and movement together to create certainty within you and build superfast empowering connections in your brain is *incantations*. These are a very powerful programming tool. You can use them for building wires and positive thought patterns about anything. In terms of our own identity, for example, what we say to ourselves is who and what we become, and powerful incantations can be used to create the identity we would like.

Begin practising incantations starting with the words 'I am ...' and then what you repeatedly tell yourself following this, with emotion and using your body, will be a powerful tool in creating the new you.

You might feel awkward doing the following exercise if you're not used to practicing incantations, but trust the process; it works. Incantations are one of the most powerful ways we can start rewiring our brains and giving clear direction to our control centre. Incantations build new programs in our minds with directed thought, repetition and changes in our body cells through movement and sound. The use of language, what you focus on and how you move your body is a powerful combination for programming your mind to create and lock in new patterns for enhanced living.

EXERCISE 11

Create Your Personal Power Incantations

Find a place where you won't be disturbed and where you can shout and jump around.

Who are you? Ask yourself who is [insert your name here]? Who do you want to be? Who WILL you be?

You know the real you, the spirited you. You know what you are capable of. You know from deep inside your soul that you were born to do great things. You know wherever you have been is preparation for who you will become and has given you invaluable lessons.

Start with the words 'I am ...' and start just randomly saying words that come to you that describe who you really are. You decide who you are, choose whatever feels right for you. You are a unique force of nature.

Here are some examples, but it can be anything you like. It's your identity.

Make a list of your own words and then start:

I am love.
I am courage.
I am joy.
I am happy.
I am free.
I am grateful.
I am powerful.
I am a force of life.
I am awesome.
I am strong.
I am giving.
I am compassionate.
I am an incredible unique gift. I am the light.
I am determined.
I am a force for good.

Now choose three of your 'I am ...' statements that you like best and make these your Personal Power Incantations.

*Shout them loudly, get animated, make a first, punch
the air, jump! If it feels weird, don't worry. Just keep doing it.
This works!*

*This is your life and you are the programmer. Make it a habit,
do it daily. Engrain it in your mind. This is your identity and
you create who you are.*

I am ... I am ... I am ...

☞ *The most powerful force of our
behaviour is being consistent
with our self-identity and we
become who we tell ourselves
we are.*

If you tell yourself 'I am stupid', or 'I am lazy', or 'I am
disorganised', or 'I am bad with money', then this self-talk
and self-imaging is forming your identity. You decide your
identity so why not decide to be great? You can create and
use incantations for anything you want to change, achieve
or become. Write them down. Put them on Post-it notes.
And most importantly, shout them loudly with emotion
and using your body. Then repeat, repeat, repeat!

Incantations can be anything you choose and this
self-direction is programming. We're generally not taught
the importance of *self-talk*, the importance of the quiet
whispers we tell ourselves or the loudest, most animated
repeated incantations.

Using uplifting language

We don't often think much about the words we use in our daily experiences, but the language we use in everything is critical to how we feel. If you ask someone how they're doing, common responses might include 'I'm doing pretty well', 'Not bad', 'Could be worse' or 'Hanging in there', or 'Getting by'. Now imagine if someone said, 'I'm feeling awesome, thank you', 'I'm on top of the world', 'Unstoppable', 'Excited', or 'I'm so grateful and happy!' The person who talks like this, using positive uplifting language, will have a very different physiology.

Would you like to feel like that? You don't have to fake it, but you can easily train yourself to feel great. The language you use, whether it's power incantations or conversation, is vitally important programming.

The great thing about using *more empowering and uplifting language* is that not only will you feel more empowered and uplifted yourself but so will those you interact with, and your words will have an impact far beyond what you can possibly imagine (more in Step 6). Who would you feel better meeting and asking how they were doing? The person with the sluggish attitude, dropped shoulders and low energy who says, 'Not too bad, I am getting by', or the person alive with energy, great posture and a smile who says, 'Really great, thank you'?

Of course, some people have physical pain to deal with and this is not all about putting on fake smiles and pretending everything is amazing, but if you focus on the language you use, you can change how you and others feel.

☞ *Even when crap is happening, you can rise above it and use empowering language to stop falling into self-pity and disempowering physiology.*

Encourage yourself and keep it fun

The language we use is critically important and nowhere more so than how we talk to ourselves. We all have internal dialogue and how we talk to ourselves will determine how we feel about ourselves. We all make mistakes, we're all learning on our journey through life on earth, and we all have things that happen which we cannot control. But what we can control is how we talk to ourselves. It seems incredible to hear people berating themselves when they make a mistake, or telling themselves they aren't good at something. Telling yourself 'I can't believe I did that, what's wrong with me', or 'I screwed up, I'm useless' is what you will come to believe.

From this moment on, think of talking to yourself as how you would talk to a child. How would a child feel if you berated them for falling over when they were learning to walk? Or for making a mistake while learning? You wouldn't be helping the child progress very well. Give yourself clear instructions, lots of encouragement and keep it fun, and you will transform your own life. Become acutely aware of how you are talking to yourself. You are human and humans learn by making mistakes.

How you talk to yourself, your internal dialogue, is building neural pathways. You are the builder, the electrician of your brain, and this is your life, so make sure you are building the most helpful pathways you can.

How you talk to yourself is critical and so too is how you see yourself. We are all making pictures and movies in our minds all the time, and our task is to become great film producers and manage the picture making we are doing so it works in the best way possible for us.

EXERCISE 12
Understand the Power of Your Imagination

Close your eyes and imagine you are walking in the blistering dry heat of the desert. You're feeling parched, your mouth is dry and you are dehydrated.

Now imagine holding a large, chilled, juicy orange and gently squeezing that into your mouth. Feel the cool liquid dropping onto your tongue.

Open your eyes. How did that make your mouth feel? Your mouth will almost certainly be watering and although this is just a simple example, it shows the power of your imagination to make physical changes.

You have only used your imagination, it's not real, and yet your body responds as if it was.

The power of visualisation

As humans we have an incredible capacity to imagine, but our minds don't know the difference between what is real and what is imagined. *Visualisation* is one of the most effective tools in training and although 'film-making in the mind' has been a training focus in high-level sport, it's now becoming much more accepted as a mainstream performance tool.

There was a piece of research conducted with basketball players in the United States where some players practised free throws and some just imagined or visualised making the free throws over and over again. When it came to them taking free throws against each other, the players who had used just visualisation performed best. In every visualisation or practice they were seeing themselves making the shot perfectly each time.

How you make pictures in your mind affects how you see yourself and what you do. Your self-image is created by you. We burden ourselves by thinking about what others might be thinking of us but we create who we are and we can't control the pictures and films others are making of us. If you have a less-than-amazing self-image, you're making a picture in your head of a less-than-amazing person. Instead, work on creating pictures in your mind of the great person you are.

If you're feeling anxious about something, which is really just 'doing' anxious thoughts (for example, maybe thinking about going into a room full of strangers and getting nervous), then you're making a movie in your head of what you imagine will happen, and it's not a very pleasant movie to watch. If you're 'doing' anxious thoughts ahead of the event, it's all made up anyway because you haven't gone into the room yet! It's your imagination and so you need to make better movies that are going to make you feel better.

EXERCISE 13

Visualising the Real Confident You

Before you go to a party, a presentation or a gathering of people you don't yet know, pause and just for a few moments imagine there is a version of you, standing just in front.

That person is compassionate, kind, funny and warm and someone people really like and want to connect with. This person is totally at ease with the situation and has a lightness and warmth that radiates from them.

Now imagine stepping forward and into that person. As you step into this version of yourself, feel what it is like to be so cool, calm and collected. See what they see, hear what they hear in that environment and feel what they feel – ready to enjoy meeting others.

This is you; this is the real person you are. You know people really want to talk with that sort of person. They are drawn to the confidence and lightness.

Now smile and enter the room with confidence and grace. Your presence speaks loudly before you have even said a word.

Visualisation is one of the most powerful techniques in mastering your mind and creating your best life. Everything is essentially created twice, first in your mind and then in your life. We need to become great film producers in our minds and direct effective pictures. We're visualising anyway, whether we are conscious of it or not, so we may as well visualise what we want and who we want to become.

> ☞ *Successful people are not playing movies in their mind of things not working out, they're making movies of what they want to happen. They are great film producers.*

Create your vision board

Practise visualisation, incorporate this technique into your life and you will change how you feel and what you do. Seeing what you want to be and how you want to behave through visualisation and then creating it in your life, is giving your powerful unconscious mind the direction it needs.

A powerful tool for creating the life you want is to create for yourself a physical vision board, a physical representation of the life you want, bringing together in visual form all your goals. You can keep this somewhere you will see it regularly and update it as you need.

You will be giving your mind *focus and instructions* on what to filter. By seeing your vision board regularly, you are reinforcing your neural pathways through repetition.

EXERCISE 14
Create Your Vision Board

Get a large board or piece of white card, big enough that you can put lots of images and notes on it. This is your vision board.

Now spend some time collating, from whatever sources you choose, images that represent the life you want so you can see the future you are going to create. Make it clear in terms of the specific areas rather than just a dump of pictures. Magazine content, photographs, internet images – whatever you can find that visually represents areas of your future life, which you are going to make real.

For example, you can have images that represent your health and fitness goals, what your financial freedom will look like, places you will travel to, spiritual growth, relationships, family, charitable goals. It's your life and your vision board so make it excite and inspire you.

Add words, draw pictures or whatever you decide will be a helpful visual representation. The more inspiring your vision board, the more it will create clarity for your unconscious mind.

When you have completed your vision board, place it somewhere you will see it regularly. This will remind you, excite you and further trigger your unconscious mind to work efficiently for you.

Replacing unhelpful pictures

Creating effective pictures in your mind is one of the most powerful skills you can develop and the better you get at this, the better your life will be. If you make unhelpful pictures, you're most likely to have an unpleasant experience. You can also give yourself more space to create effective pictures by clearing away some of the old negative ones.

When you visualise, if you are making films or recalling memories that you don't like, imagine yourself stepping out of the film and observing it. It happened in the past so you're able to be an observer. Once you're outside the film, you can do what you like with the pictures. You can pause, rewind, scramble, dull the colour, mute the sound and push it far away or just dissolve the redundant film you don't like. When the film is one you really like, you can stay in the film and feel, see and hear as vividly as you can, amplifying all the sensory inputs. This simple technique of *immersing yourself* in movies you like and *extracting yourself* and changing films you don't, is a useful technique in your armoury of tools for managing your mental imagery and storage.

EXERCISE 15
Wash Your Mind

Is there something that happened in the past that you spend a lot of time thinking about and which doesn't make you feel good? Most people have something, or lots of things!

How much of your life is spent thinking about this? How much time is eaten up with thoughts about this? Do you think about it daily, weekly, monthly? Even a couple of hours a day can add up to over 30 days every year just thinking about this thing!

When you think about the event/person that is distressing, you are really just watching a film of this in your mind.

Now think about this film you are watching. Where is that film playing? What size is it? Is it moving? Is it in colour?

When we focus on past events that are making us not feel great, usually we are seeing a big moving film, close up, in colour and with sounds. It is very real in our mind so it is causes us to feel bad.

So, as you think about the event that causes you to have distressing thoughts, watch the movie and then imagine condensing it into a bundle of pictures or a video file.

Now take that compressed file and move it further away from you, shrink it down, drain all the colour and sound out of it and now zap it away in a puff of smoke with a click of your fingers.

It may seem strange if you're not used to doing this, but keep practising and you'll become much more aware of these films playing in your mind and you'll find it easy to use the technique of managing unhelpful, time-eating memories.

Become more aware of the movies you are watching, get rid of the crap ones and make great new ones. It's as simple as that.

Understanding your unconscious mind

The terms 'brain' and 'mind' are often used interchangeably, but they are different . The brain is a physical organ, a processor. It's our hardware, we know exactly where it's located and we understand a lot about its physical properties. The mind, however, includes the *output* of the brain's activities, and is invisible within us, including our thoughts, beliefs, self-talk and imagination. While it has been usual to think of the mind as being just in the brain, our mind is really within our whole body. It's in every cell of who we are.

We process information from the world around us through our senses in images, sounds, smells, tastes and feelings, and we represent this processed information internally. There are a lot of stimuli so the brain works to generalise, delete and distort based on what we have already experienced. It would be impossible to process everything, so we have to filter.

When we're thinking, we're primarily creating pictures and sounds and recalling memories or using our imagination. Because of the volume and complexity of information we need to process, and the functions we need to manage, our mind operates on two levels: the conscious level which we are aware of, and a level below the surface, which we are not consciously aware of, our unconscious.

The conscious mind is easy to understand and you are using it now to read this. It's able to deal with up to nine ideas or experiences at any one time. The unconscious mind, however, is limitless. Everything we have ever seen, heard, smelled, tasted and felt are stored in our unconscious mind. It also stores patterns of programming or learning which enable us to do a lot of things without being consciously aware.

When we learn a new skill, like riding a bike or driving a car, we first learn with our conscious mind and then the learning goes into our unconscious mind so we can perform without consciously being aware of the actions that enable us to perform the task at hand. The unconscious mind also controls our heartbeat, breathing and many other functions that run the human body. We would otherwise be completely overwhelmed and it would be impossible to be conscious of everything, so our unconscious mind runs most of what is going on. For example, when the information about driving is stored in your unconscious mind, it is stored like software that can be run automatically whenever needed. It's your autopilot.

EXERCISE 16
Build Awareness of Your Unconscious Mind

Wherever you are reading this, just for a moment touch your nose with your right hand.

Now relax. That was very simple, wasn't it?

You probably did this very easily and quickly, but can you explain what happened in order for you to do this? It's quite a remarkable sequence of actions involving muscles, ligaments, feelings and memory, all just to do something like this very simple task, but your unconscious mind did this easily for you.

You could do any amount of other body-moving actions of various complexity, but hopefully you've already understood just from this simple example that your unconscious mind is your autopilot working for you based on the programming, or instructions you have already installed.

Our conscious mind learns by logic and repetition and our unconscious mind stores and takes direction and suggestion, being most receptive when it's in a relaxed state. It is easier to programme when the mind isn't distracted by external stimuli. The patterns that our unconscious mind is already running can be helpful, but there are also patterns of programming which may not help us, especially in areas of belief, values and habits. If, for example, you really want to be in a fulfilling relationship, but your unconscious mind is programmed to be scared of commitment, then you'll unconsciously be looking for people you don't have to commit to. You may have built an unconscious wall to protect yourself, but it will also imprison you. Or if you believe all the best people have been taken, then you'll be unconsciously looking for 'what's wrong' with everyone you meet.

Quieting the mind

We need to create *new programmes for our unconscious mind* to replace unhelpful or limiting ones and align our conscious thoughts with our unconscious ones to give a clear direction. Meditation, mindfulness and hypnosis are all great practices to help us manage our minds. All are about quieting the mind and lessening external stimulation so the brain can focus. Don't worry too much about the labels. What is important is that they are all tools to quieten the mind.

> *Everyone should meditate for 20 minutes a day. If you are too busy you should meditate for an hour.*

Zen saying

When we put our mind into a less distracted state it's much more susceptible to suggestions and taking instructions. These mind-quieting practices have been going on as long as people have been sitting calmly with their eyes shut, but now the benefits of *meditation*, *mindfulness* and *hypnosis* are increasingly backed by science.

 A quieter, more focused mind, one that is looking in rather than out, is going to be more efficient and open than a busy distracted mind.

EXERCISE 17
Quieten Your Mind

Sit comfortably and quietly. When you are relaxed, think about your breathing.

Breathe in deeply and exhale slowly, noticing every breath. Keep breathing in and out, slow deep breaths from the diaphragm.

Now let your mind just wander where it wants, and as you do, it will have lots of thoughts. That's how it operates. It generates thoughts, it runs patterns and processes. Observe these thoughts, but keep returning to your breath.

Enjoy feeling calm and relaxed, with each breath out releasing all tension and stress from your body, and with each inhale bringing fresh, new, energised oxygen to your body.

You're already experiencing having more mind control because when you focus on your breathing you can't also be aware of having other thoughts at the same time. When you take your focus away from your breathing, however, you'll become aware of your thoughts again.

Focus again on your breathing and just quietly say 'thank you' with each exhale. You don't need to be conscious of being thankful for anything in particular, just repeat as you breathe out: 'Thank you, thank you, thank you'.

This is a very simple example of an exercise to quieten the mind and there are many ways you can practice mind calming. The essence is to keep returning to your breath, know you have control of what you focus on, and that your thoughts are just thoughts.

Our limiting beliefs

We often know what we want to do, but we have invisible blocks, such as limiting beliefs, values and habits. These are *reinforced unconscious patterns* that cause unhelpful thoughts and feelings preventing us from taking effective action. This unconscious programming drives how we feel and what we do. We can know what to do but we need our conscious and unconscious to be aligned if we are going to take the action necessary to change.

Beliefs are the lenses through which we interpret the world and our experiences, and they colour everything that we say and think. They are just reinforced patterns in our brain mostly based on memories and experiences.

We aren't born with any beliefs, we form them. Beliefs are the neural pathways that have become entrenched and that we believe with certainty based on our experiences and programming from our environment. These beliefs, and entrenched pathways, often remain unexamined through people's lives. One of the biggest problems is that people don't realise that their beliefs are only beliefs. If we were taught this from an early age, there likely would be a lot less conflict and war in the world. It's important to be aware of our beliefs and ask whether they are limiting or disempowering us in our pursuit of the life we want. If they are limiting us, we need to destroy them and replace them with empowering ones.

We all have some beliefs that limit us and these are usually, to some degree, thinking we're not enough in some area of life, such as 'I'm not young enough', 'not old enough', 'not smart enough', 'not attractive enough', 'not educated enough', 'not rich enough'.

At their core, limiting beliefs are about our deepest fear, which is that we aren't enough, and if we aren't enough, that we won't be loved. However, if we're aware of these unhelpful beliefs, which are blocking us, we can crush them and replace them with new, empowering beliefs and unleash our limitless power.

> *Our life is the creation of our mind.*

Buddha

We already know from earlier in the chapter that to make new, superfast 'broadband' pathways, we need to link emotion and movement to wire this into our bodies.

To crush a limiting belief, we need to replace the old unhelpful belief with a new empowering one, which is usually the opposite, and build a superfast pathway to it.

EXERCISE 18
Crush Your Limiting Beliefs

Read this exercise. Then re-read it. Make sure you really understand the instructions before you start.

When you're ready, think of a belief you have that's limiting you. (We all have some of these, so don't kid yourself and pretend you don't have any!) Focus now on this limiting belief you have chosen and as you think of it, close your eyes and imagine what it would it be like to hang onto this belief as you carry on through life.

Think of the pain it will cause, what you'll miss out on in life, who you'll miss, and the effect it will have on those around you.

The impact is likely to be huge. Go deep and imagine the 'cost' to your life in five years. Think about what your life would look like if you still had that limiting belief after all that time. How would that feel?

Now go even further to ten years in your future with the same beliefs, and what it would cost you in a decade.

Keep going, for another ten years, that's 20 years from now. What is your life going to be like in 20 years if you hang onto this, and other, limiting beliefs? That's 20 years of limiting your life because of a belief you have installed as software in your mind.

The more vividly and intensely you imagine being in the future with this limiting belief, the more effective the exercise will be, as your body, mind and soul really need to associate the pain that will be caused by living with the same old belief.

Can you change? Can you get out of that pain? You must decide, and if you have done the exercise correctly you will be in no doubt that you cannot hold onto that limiting belief any longer, that belief which will cause so much pain for the rest of your life.

When you've reached a point of imagining the pain as so unbearable, decide to say 'No, this is bullshit!' Tell yourself you don't want that pain; you refuse to accept the pain and the damage it causes. You can change and you will change and you will change now!

Having decided to eliminate this unhelpful blocking belief, now all you need to do is install a new empowering belief in place of the now crushed limiting one. This new empowering belief will usually be the opposite of the old limiting belief.

With the new empowering belief, now imagine yourself in five, ten and 20 years and what your life will look like with this new belief. How will you feel? Who will be in your life? How different will your life be?

Once you have installed the new belief, you can revisit your old limiting belief and laugh at the absurdity of the old crap programming you were holding on to. You can shout as an incantation your new belief in the old, limiting belief's place, if that helps. You know you have reprogrammed yourself and your unconscious mind is unlocked.

You decide what you believe. *You* control your life and *you* create your future. Being aware of what is holding you back, what unhelpful beliefs you've been holding onto and knowing how to change these, is a huge part of your personal growth.

Identify your values

Based on what we believe and our experiences in life, we all learn that there are some feelings or emotional states that we value more than others. There are feelings that we want to have more of in our lives and feelings we want to experience less of, or move away from. These are our values and, alongside our beliefs, they are a guiding force for everything we do. But are we aware of these values and whether they are working for the life we want?

We all want to move towards certain values and away from others, but often there's a conflict. For example, can you be really successful and liked by everyone? The idea is to understand your values, in other words what's important to you. Your brain works to put things in a hierarchy, so whether we are aware or not, we have values and we prioritise them. We have probably never stopped to study our values, but when we become more aware, we can consciously choose the values we want ordered in the hierarchy we want and we can make sure there are no conflicts. Once we have done this, we can then make superhighway neural pathways to these feel-good values, and narrow or erase the pathways to values we want to avoid.

EXERCISE 19
Assess Your Values

Start with a clean sheet of paper and draw a line down the middle.

What's really important to you? What feelings are you trying to pursue and what makes you feel that way?

On the left-hand side of the line make a list of these emotional states that you value most in life. They could be, for example, freedom, justice, growth, joy, vitality, etc. Write down anything you feel you want to write down. Five or six words is enough.

When you have finished making this list, make another list on the right-hand side of the line of everything you are trying to avoid or don't like in terms of your feelings. This could include, for example, injustice, frustration, anger, jealousy, envy, etc.

Remember, these feelings, both good and bad, are yours and yours alone.

We're not trying to make an exhaustive list, so just write down what comes to you.

Now you should have two lists. Label them, simply as your 'towards values' on the left-hand side and your 'away from values' on the right.

You can refine these lists and the values as you grow at any time, but the key is to be aware of the top values that are steering your life, and most importantly to examine if any potentially conflict with each other. If your top values are, for example, adventure and also security, you will have an in-built conflict in your operational programming.

Bringing your values into your consciousness, examining them and working to rearrange them to work for you in alignment is a critical part of realising your potential and feeling really fulfilled in life. This is what the exercise is all about.

Become more aware of your values and understand the order in which you are prioritising them.

You are in the director's chair and now you can organise your values to propel yourself forward rather than feel conflicted or blocked.

All success starts in your mind and you have all the tools in this chapter, Step 2 of the SYSO System, to become your own great neuro manager. Be the director of your mind, control how you think and you can change your life. Install better programmes. You have learnt some great mind-management exercises in this Step and like all exercises, you need to commit to repeating these and practising. You don't become fit and strong by going to the gym only once; the training, and growing, *never stops*.

> *Nourish the mind like you would your body. The mind cannot survive on junk food.*

Brian Tracy

STEP 3
Take Charge of Your Emotions

You cannot always control what goes on outside, but you can always control what goes on inside.

Wayne Dyer

The quality of your life really boils down to how you feel emotionally. This is the *flavouring of your experiences*. You could be a billionaire and yet feel frustrated, angry, guilty, envious, bitter and full of regrets. Or you could be stone-cold broke but feel inspired, excited about the future, grateful and full of laughter and love for life. Which would you rather be?

Well, the good news is you don't have to choose, as life isn't an either/or game between areas of achievement and fulfilment. Although we strive to achieve things like great relationships and optimum health, it's really just the feelings these things give us that we are seeking.

We tend to be striving for things outside ourselves, but it's really our internal world that will determine how we feel. Working on our internal world is the key to living our best life. Happiness is not dictated by circumstances. As you know from Step 2, it is electric and chemical reactions within you and you can manage these to choose exactly how you would like to feel.

> *When pain, misery or anger happens. It is time to look within you, not around you.*

Sadhguru

What is emotion?

What is this thing we call emotion anyway and where does it come from? Most psychologists, therapists and self-help programmes use long lists of words to describe different defined emotions that they believe exist inside us, such as anger, grief, disgust, joy, sadness, apathy, shock, guilt, jealousy, shame, envy, remorse and sadness, among many others. Some believe that there are a small number of core emotions and that all other emotions derive from these. Others focus their explanations on a belief that there are different emotions, which mix together in the same way an artist mixes primary colours to create other colours.

Ultimately, whether there are four, six, eight, 27 or 34,000 emotions (and yes, there are psychologists who believe there are those specific numbers of emotions), according to these theories, every emotion exists within all of us all the time, just waiting to be triggered. The idea behind these approaches is usually about becoming more aware of these different emotions and labelling them so we can identify when they are triggered.

But how can we know which emotion is which? When something doesn't go the way we want, are we experiencing anger or frustration or disappointment, or is it a mix of all these? No matter how many labels there are, it could be quite stressful just trying to work out which emotion is which! And does it matter anyway? When we think of emotions as separate, defined, specific feelings inside us, the number of emotions we have is limited only by the number of different words we can come up with to describe any small difference in feeling.

Psychologists also like to categorise different emotions as either positive or negative. If we're going to master our emotions, this would mean we, not only have to define and label everything we feel, but on top of that, we need to classify each emotion as positive or negative. Even if we subscribe to the theory that there are different distinguishable emotions, can each really be classified as either negative or positive? It is how these emotions are working for us that would determine whether something is helpful or unhelpful, rather than the emotion itself. It would be dependent on context, on the situation. For example anger, frustration and fear are potentially really helpful to us in the right situation.

If you were walking home alone down a dark alley and you suddenly noticed a group of people shouting and armed with knives, would a feeling of fear be helpful to you? Of course it would. Your body would move into a more alert state and you would decide to get away as soon as possible. If you were getting frustrated because something didn't feel right in one of your relationships or at college, could this be a helpful signal that something needs to be changed? It would be a really good cue for action, in that context.

☞ *Feelings inside us are signals,
so listening to how we feel
is invaluable for our growth,
and developing a higher
awareness of this internal
world of emotion is at the
heart of effective personal
development.*

Energy in motion

What if we don't have emotions waiting within us to be
triggered? What if we don't have distinct separate emotions
within us at all? What if we just have energy that is in
motion, which is actually the origin of the word e-*motion*?
Rather than having lots of different emotions within us,
we have electricity and chemicals which get activated to
cause feelings. We think thoughts that cause chemicals to be
released in our bodies, and electrical movements of energy
within us, which working together constitute our feeling.

We don't have anger within us, we have angry thoughts
that release chemicals which change how we feel and which
stimulate our electricity or energy flow. This flow creates a
particular feeling. We can have joyful thoughts that release
chemicals, which stimulate our energy flow in a different
way and which causes a different feeling. We can have any

feeling we choose as we decide the label to put on that feeling. Every time you believe you are triggering a particular emotion, think instead about energy moving within you rather than it being a specific labelled emotion, which has just been activated.

As you will see in more detail in Step 7, we are all just energy. Life is energy and we know from Step 2 that our brain processing is basically just electricity and chemicals, and chemicals can cause various chemical reactions to create further energy. Life is energy flowing, and it flows in waves.

EXERCISE 20
Take Charge of Your Energy in Motion

Consider for a moment something in your life that causes you to have angry thoughts when you think about it. It could be a breach of trust, an injustice or an occasion where you were taken advantage of.

Whatever it is, think about it really intensely now, as if you are right there in the moment when this happened. As you think about it, become more aware of how it makes you feel.

Does it feel like there is movement within your body? Is there an intensity you feel somewhere as you think about it? There will be a response in your body somehow; you just have to start being more aware of what, and where, this is.

Each of us will experience the intensity differently but mostly it is likely to be a rising feeling or a deep feeling in our gut or chest area, like waves or a strong flow of energy spinning.

Your energy has been activated to move within you in a certain way (electricity) by your thoughts and the neurotransmitters (chemicals), depending on how you were thinking about the event/person/happening and the meaning you've attached to it. Now think about which way this energy flow is moving or rising in your body.

As you feel it, decide you are going to move it the other way, or spin it in the opposite direction.

If you have followed the instructions correctly, you'll be feeling different from when you started the exercise. You will have consciously taken charge of, and changed, the way the energy moves within you and it will also feel less intense.

I don't want to be at the mercy of my emotions, I want to use them, to enjoy them, and to dominate them.

Oscar Wilde

What you have experienced in the exercise is simply being conscious of the energy within you, the energy in motion and how you can control the way it flows with your thinking. This energy is the same *life force* that is always within you, it just moves or gets stirred up in different ways and in different intensities depending primarily on the thoughts you have and the chemicals those thoughts release. The principle is the same for all your thoughts and the energy will flow depending on the intensity of how much you like or dislike what you are thinking about.

Your ocean of emotion

 Your emotion within you is like the ocean, and you can decide and take charge of how you want that energy flow to be moving.

You can become aware of your ocean of emotion rising or subsiding. You can feel it within you moving and you can choose to either fan it and stir it up, by continuing with similar thoughts, or to control it.

Imagine you're floating in the ocean and the water stirs up with a storm and the waves get wild. The water moves fast, and smashes against the shoreline. On the other hand, imagine the calm rocking of the water and the waves gently lapping on the shoreline. Imagine something quite dramatic happens in your life that you didn't want to happen.
If you're aware and in charge, you can feel the energy in motion building and if you decide to change your thoughts and take charge, you can control your ocean of emotion and, you can prevent the wild seas from causing havoc.

You can't control the events, but you can control the weather patterns because these are controlled by your thinking.
The question is what kind of weather would you like?
Two people can experience the same event, but if one person thinks of it is as really bad and negative, while another thinks of it as actually quite positive, their thoughts, and the intensity of those thoughts, will be very different and will determine how their energy moves.

It's not the load that breaks you down, it's the way you carry it.

Lou Holtz

Practise gratitude

One of the most powerful thinking tools you have available
to you at all times is *gratitude*, which alone is one of the
quickest ways to change how you stir emotion within you.
When you have grateful thoughts, you'll be unable to think
of anything negative at the same time. Try it! You can't be
angry when you're being grateful. You can't feel frustrated
when you're being grateful. Gratitude is your number one
tool for taking charge of your emotions or changing the
energy flow within you. Practise gratitude and not only will
you feel differently, the more you practise, the more you'll
realise there's a lot to be grateful for!

Manage your fire

Another way of looking at energy in motion within you is
to think of it as a fire; you can decide to fan the flames or
let it burn out. You're the fire officer for your own fires and
you have all the equipment you need on hand at any time
inside you to decide how much fire you would like. You might
not be able to completely control the triggers for the fires –
although you will get better at this with practise – but you
can observe this energy feeling within you and then decide if
you would like to let it burn out if it is unhelpful, or fuel it to
burn more if it's helpful.

When my young children have their own little raging
emotions from not getting what they want, my wife and

I let them burn off steam and calm down before we do anything. It takes a little time for the energy to change and normal communication to continue. Distractions and thought pattern changes can speed this up, but the stronger the energy charge, the longer it takes to calm. It's the same for all of us at all ages, it's just much more obvious in a two-year-old child as they haven't yet learnt to try and disguise how they feel.

As you build your awareness and realise that you're in charge, not only will you experience fewer fires, but you will also know that you can manage them by either fanning them, if they are feelings you want more of, or letting them burn out, if they are feelings you want less of. Knowing you have this power over your feelings is an inner strength and will give you the freedom of being able to choose how you want to feel.

We have talked mostly about thoughts triggering chemicals and energy flow as this is the main way your energy flow is affected, but there are other things that can also affect the electricity and chemicals released in your body. What we put into or bodies, such as food and drugs, and external energy waves, such as from the weather, music or electromagnetic activity, will affect how our electricity and chemicals flow. How you *move* also affects your energy and chemicals, which is one of the reasons why you feel so good when you exercise.

The power of breath

How you breathe is one of the most underrated capabilities we have that affects how we feel; with every breath, we stimulate millions of cells in our respiratory system and when we change our breathing patterns, we change the messages we send to our brain and the energy flow and chemicals released. Breathing is a hugely important factor in how we feel and if we build more awareness about how we breathe, we can practise breathing techniques to manage our emotion. When you focus on your breathing, you can't be focusing on unhelpful thoughts, and there are physiologically relaxing, scientifically proven benefits from breathing practices. When people talk about having panic attacks, this is usually due to someone forgetting to breathe. So in moments of intense emotion, breathe deeply and you'll immediately start calming your ocean of emotion, and releasing physical tension too.

EXERCISE 21
Practise Breathing Awareness

Make yourself comfortable somewhere quiet, either standing or sitting.

Take ten slow, long, extra-deep breaths, inhaling and exhaling for five or six seconds each time, breathing in through your nose and out through your mouth. These should be big, diaphragmic breaths where you really feel your chest and upper body expand with each inhale, and deflate with each exhale.

Imagine inhaling new positivity and vitality with each breath in, and imagine you're getting rid of any negativity, unhelpful thoughts and rubbish in your mind with each deep breath out. Each breath is quite literally changing your life.

Pause after a set of ten breaths, then return to breathing in a normal, relaxed state and just be still.

In this stillness, focus your awareness on the energy within you. Be grateful for this energy flow and for knowing you're in control of this ocean of energy in motion that you are.

Now repeat the deep diaphragmic breaths with two more sets of ten, pausing and focusing again on your energy awareness between each set.

How you breathe is a critical component of your emotional state and there are many breathing techniques you can learn to help you change how you feel. Breathing is a fascinating and essential part of our life, yet learning how we can breathe differently to manage our state gets little attention in conventional education. If you practice yoga or similar activities, you should already be very aware of your breathing and techniques to influence how you feel.

What are you watching?

In Step 2 we looked at how when we think about something we're mostly creating pictures or a movie in our mind, and the type of movie you make will determine how you stir the emotional energy within you. Are you stoking and fanning your fires of good feelings, like love, joy, excitement, when you create images in your mind? Are you making sure any less desirable states, like anger and frustration, are fizzling out and dissipating? You are in charge of what you fan or extinguish. *You are the manager of your energy.* You can decide what movies to watch.

EXERCISE 22
Manage the Pictures in your Mind

Think of something that really makes you annoyed. It could be anything. When you think about it, you have frustrated and angry thoughts.

What are you seeing and hearing in your mind when you think of this?

From Step 2, you know that when you think of something you are creating pictures in your mind, and you can change the pictures and the way you are looking at them to change the way you feel.

What picture do you see? Is the image large or small, close to you or far away? Is the image in colour or black and white? Moving or still? Loud or quiet?

Become more aware of the detail in your pictures and know that you can manage these images, and produce different ones if the current ones aren't working for you.

Draw a border around this picture that is making you annoyed.

When it has its border, shrink it right down, drain the colour, move it far away and turn the sound down. This is often called 'changing the sub-modalities'.

Adjusting these aspects of your imagining allows you to disempower the images that are annoying you, which subsequently causes different electric and chemical charges within you.

You are the manager and producer of what you choose to watch and how you choose to feel.

Try the exercise again, but now also replace old, unhelpful pictures with more helpful and fun pictures.

Make better pictures and movies and you'll feel better. It's as simple as that. You are the producer and director of your own mind art and mind movies so you can decide to watch anything you choose.

Much of the processing is happening in our unconscious mind so it's critical that we are managing and programming our mind using the tools we suggested in Step 2 .

The impact of fear

Think of something that makes you fearful. Fear is usually thought of in a negative way but, as we said earlier, fear can be incredibly useful in life and is part of our *survival* nature, helping raise awareness of, or encouraging us to remove ourselves from, dangerous and harmful situations. When we think fearful thoughts, our body increases its heartbeat and respiration rate in order to provide the energy and oxygen that will be needed to fuel a rapid response to perceived danger. Blood flow to the surface areas of the body is reduced and the flow to the muscles, brain, legs and arms is increased. The body prepares itself to be more aware and alert during times of danger with the dilation of the pupils, which allows more light into the eyes, and your muscles become tense and primed for action, which can result in trembling or shaking. That's a lot of natural physiological change just from some fearful thoughts.

We should be grateful for the feelings we have that alert us, but fearful thoughts can also sometimes be debilitating, irrational and stop us from doing stuff we really want to do. Fear is essentially imagining a bad outcome for something that hasn't happened yet. Phobias are excessive and irrational thoughts. We can change how we think, to change how we feel and get rid of these irrational fears by creating more helpful pictures in our minds. The most common excessive fears include fears of flying, spiders, rats, public speaking and heights.

Irrational fear

Rational fear we know is helpful. For example, you wouldn't want to get too close to an edge with a huge drop, and staying away from rats is generally a good idea so as not to catch disease, but phobias can hold us back. With phobias, the mind has created a movie which affects the energy flow and physiological responses in a particularly debilitating way, but if we just change the movies that we're playing to ourselves, we'll change how we feel and how we react.

Estimates suggest as many as 25% of adults are scared of flying. When someone is scared of flying, what movie do you think they're making when they take a flight? Are they thinking how confined they are? Are they imagining the plane falling out of the sky and all the passengers dying? Whatever the specifics, they're likely to be making a movie in their mind of all the terrible things they imagine could go wrong. How is that going to make their energy flow? With phobias, it's just the thought of flying that causes the image, not actually getting on a plane, and those who suffer with phobias are very good at making vivid movies about something that hasn't happed yet. They are making it up, or imagining the worst and they are actually very good movie-makers.

What if they made an equally vivid movie, but this time focusing on a much better outcome? Perhaps picturing themselves relaxing, having some well-deserved 'me time' and being waited on as they choose what to do. A time to be calm, read, watch a documentary, a time to plan and to think about the excitement ahead. What energy reaction is that kind of movie going to create?

EXERCISE 23
Dealing with Irrational Fear

If you are 'doing' excessive fearful thinking to the level it is debilitating, try this simple process of breathing and more helpful movie making.

Start with breathing; take deeper breaths to relax from tension and change your energy flow. You can change the depth and pace of your breaths as we have already done in previous exercises. Enjoy the feeling of release when you exhale after a long deep inhale.

When you are experiencing fear, you're thinking fearful thoughts as you play a movie in your mind that reinforces these thoughts and which causes your energy to move in a particular way.

Now imagine something specific that you're really fearful of. It could be flying, seeing spiders or public speaking. It doesn't matter.

Notice the movie this triggers and then step out of the movie and imagine you're watching it on a large cinema screen. See yourself sitting, relaxed in your cinema armchair. You're watching the film, rather than being in it.

Imagine you have a remote-control device in your hand to manage how the movie plays.

When you are ready, press the pause button. Take a few deep breaths and then fast forward to the end. It is a boring and unhelpful film you've played many times so let's get to the end. Pause when you arrive at the end frame.

Now press fast rewind and watch the film rewind back. Notice how it's scrambled and how all the colour and sound is draining from it. When it reaches the beginning, it has virtually faded away and it culminates in a final little puff of smoke and disappears into the distance.

You have erased the film, and are now able to produce a much more helpful one.

Play a new film, one that you create, where you're in control. Visualise yourself calmly doing what you previously feared. It feels so much better. At the end of your new film, pause and celebrate.

Now you know how to erase crap films and make new ones. It's all in your imagination! Your mind is in your control, so make great films. Why watch rubbish ones?

You can repeat this process as often as you like. The key point is to step out of the unhelpful film and watch yourself in it, pressing the fast forward and then the rewind scramble until it becomes drained and disappears in a puff of smoke.

Physiological responses

At some point, you will have felt your stomach churn or your heart palpitate from anxious thoughts. These *physiological responses*, such as sweaty palms or a racing heartbeat, are regulated by your nervous system. The most basic of these physiological changes are associated with the upper chest area, and are likely to correspond to changes in breathing and heart rate, but there are lots of changes in our bodies that occur as a result of our thoughts. The autonomic nervous system controls involuntary body responses, such as blood flow and digestion, whereas the sympathetic nervous system is charged with controlling the body's 'fight or flight' reactions.

When you are facing a threat, these responses automatically prepare your body to either flee from danger or face the threat. Brain scans have shown that a tiny almond-shaped structure in the brain, the amygdala, plays an important role in stirring emotion from fearful thoughts in particular.

Brain imaging has been used to show that when people are shown threatening images, the amygdala becomes activated. A network of neural pathways connects the amygdala to the other parts of the brain, allowing us to reflect on our feelings and to think before acting. In times of perceived crisis, however, those pathways are bypassed and impulse overrides reason with a kind of emotional hijacking in which the amygdala takes over the brain. It's therefore wise to be mindful of your emotional state if conversations get heated.

Angry thoughts flood the brain with catecholamines, which are hormones that prime the body for action and stimulate the nervous system, putting it on a general state of alert. Someone who is already in a bad mood will remain edgy and more easily aroused to anger than someone who is not, so it's smart to be tuned into your energy in motion, your electricity and chemicals, and take charge of dissipating any unhelpful feelings to bring your ocean of emotion back to a calmer state.

There is a chain of rapidly occurring reactions inside the body when someone is 'doing' angry thoughts, helping to mobilise the body's resources to deal with threatening circumstances. This results in an increase in heart rate, blood pressure, and breathing rate. After the threat is gone, it can take between 20 and 60 minutes for the body to return to its pre-arousal levels.

> *Make a speech when you are angry and it will be the best speech you will ever regret.*

Anonymous

EXERCISE 24
Adopt the Two-minute Rule

You understand it is inevitable that many things in life will simply not go your way.

However, agree from this moment that you are only ever going to allow yourself to feel bad for two minutes at any time. Rather than unrealistically saying 'I'm never going to feel crap', just put a limit on it and know that you are in control.

Anytime you become aware you are doing angry thoughts, focus on the feelings this thinking is causing. You now understand what is happening and the storm of energy in motion that will be starting to build.

Acknowledge it, be grateful for its intention even if it's not necessary, and then let it fizzle out by focusing on your breathing and controlling the process.

You can change how you feel with techniques like breathing differently, moving, or changing focus so you are in the control seat. You decide. And two minutes is more than enough time to allow yourself to feel crap, don't you think?

You already own the best medicine

According to the American Medical Association, stress contributes to around 75% of all cases of illnesses in the United States. Your body *changes* physically due to the chemicals released by any stressful thoughts. For example, your blood pressure goes up when you have angry thoughts and your heart rate rises when you have fearful thoughts. Taking charge of your emotions is one of the best medicines, has no negative side effects, is free and doesn't require an appointment with a doctor.

In Step 2 , we looked at how our brain processes information through our senses, and it is no coincidence our sensory organs are located near our brain. Your brain processes all the information it receives based on your previous experiences and the values and beliefs you have programmed, and it thinks thoughts. The thinking processes release chemicals, which cause reactions. Although there are many recipes of chemicals and these are changing all the time in our dynamic biochemistry, the actual biological function of all these chemicals is complex and multifaceted, affecting numerous physiological processes. There is lots you can read about biochemistry, but for the purposes of the SYSO System and changing your life, you don't need to know everything, it's just useful to have a basic understanding of some key chemicals, and most importantly to know what you can do to manage your biochemistry for the feelings you want.

Dopamine is the chemical responsible for reward-driven behaviour and pleasure seeking. In simple terms, if you want to get a hit of feel-good dopamine, set a goal and achieve it. Dopamine brings feelings of pleasure based on a certain action, and every time a response to something results in a reward, *the pathways and associations between brain cells* become stronger by increasing the intensity at which they respond to particular stimuli.

Another chemical, serotonin, is involved in mood and perception, although it plays many different roles in our bodies. It's like the body's natural tranquiliser; it relaxes us, regulates body temperature and appetite, sets our internal clock for sleep, and makes us feel peaceful and contented.

Oxytocin is another feel-good chemical messenger and is directly linked to human connection and bonding. New parents, particularly mothers, get a big hit of oxytocin when their child is born. Also called the 'love hormone', oxytocin is believed to make people feel close and contented, and their hearts calm.

Endorphins, the next group of chemicals, are associated with feelings of pleasure and with pain relief and the name endorphin means 'self-produced morphine'. Endorphins are produced during strenuous physical exertion and in many ways, they are natural painkillers and soothers.

Endocannabinoids are increasingly called the 'bliss molecules' and it may be that they are more specifically responsible for what we call 'runner's high'. Gamma-aminobutyric acid (GABA) is a molecule that slows down the firing of neurons and creates a sense of calmness. You can produce this naturally by practising yoga or meditation, for example.

Adrenaline is like an energy molecule and plays a large role in our human fight or flight mechanism; its release is exhilarating and creates a surge in energy. It causes an increase in heart rate and blood pressure and works by constricting less important blood vessels to increase blood flow to larger muscles. An adrenaline 'rush' comes in times of distress or fear but it can be triggered on demand by doing, or imagining, things that scare you or feel dangerous.

These are just some of the more commonly referred-to neurochemicals, and not only are there many, many more, they'll be released in different strengths and different blends with other chemicals. The important point is that these chemicals affect how you feel, and you can create and manage them by controlling your thinking.

Once you're aware of what's happening with your neurochemicals and how these are influenced by thoughts, you can catch yourself earlier and manage the chemical responses and feelings you have better. What and how we think causes so many changes in our body and this has a big knock-on effect. You can also use this to your advantage by being proactive about managing your thinking, you can consciously prime your body – using breath and movement – to be better *prepared to perform* in any situation.

By now you should be starting to see that emotion and chemical changes in your body are human resources available to help you, but that you need to take charge and control these if you want them to work for you in the best way possible. Emotion is electrical and biochemical. It's all about your body and it could be that your thoughts and feelings occur not just in the brain, as has been traditionally thought, but in virtually every system and cell of your body, which is all inextricably linked in your nervous system. Thoughts are translated into chemical expressions, or 'codes', by our bodies, and are then communicated through our various intimately connected body systems. It's therefore no surprise that there is increasing emphasis on the interaction of mind and body in health studies and medicine.

Movement and music

One of the most important things we can do to release chemicals in our bodies, to change how the energy travels and how we feel, is to move. Movement and exercise cause chemicals to be released and also wakes up your cells. You're likely to be aware of feeling good when you have exercised. Apart from stimulating your cells, when you exercise you release endorphins, dopamine and serotonin which creates a great cocktail of feel-good chemicals. Moving your body is vitally important in how you feel and if you're experiencing any unhelpful emotions, exercise is a good place to start.

Emotion and chemicals are also stimulated through each of your senses. For example, we all know music has the potential to change how we feel and in Step 1 we learnt that music is made up of pressure waves and that different waves can makes us feel differently. Music has often been called the 'sound of our emotions' and this may be an accurate representation. The waves affect our energy in motion and the thoughts we have when we process lyrics, together with patterns of vibrations, release chemicals.

Additionally, what we see, such as art and nature, and what we taste and touch, can change our biochemistry and energy flows. Taken altogether, we have plenty of tools to change how we feel at any time and to take charge of our emotional responses. Whether it's how we think, how we move, listening to music, eating, drinking, tactile experiences, looking at nature or art, smelling perfume or flowers; all these stimulations cause electric and chemical reactions.

Moreover, research is increasingly proving that emotion affects our immunity. By being in charge of our energy flow we can increase our resistance to disease and stay healthier for longer. Feel good and live longer! Pretty compelling reasons to take charge of your natural chemicals, don't you think?

Choose how you want to feel

Emotional energy is different at different times and it *ebbs and flows*, but the principle remains the same. Our chemistry changes and our senses change, but we can still decide at any time how we want to feel. Having that power within yourself is about the most liberating thing you can feel. Never again buy into excuses like 'my emotions got the better of me'.

 Choose how you want to feel and know you are running your emotions, not the other way around.

We now know that instead of thinking of different specific emotions existing within us, it's much more helpful to think of emotion as the energy within us, which moves primarily in relation to our thoughts and our physiology.

We are in control, not at the mercy of our emotion, and we don't have to label differences in this energy movement. Instead, start examining the type of thoughts we have. We've discussed that emotion flowing through your body is just electricity and chemicals, and you can specifically condition yourself to be in charge of this emotional energy to work for you. You're still going to experience crap in your life which will make you feel bad and push your energy in motion in unhelpful ways; the key is that when you're in charge, you can let it burn out quickly and not let it engulf you. You can catch your unhelpful processes much quicker and deal with them earlier before the fire gets out of hand. Being aware gives you the power to decide how you will feel and to take control of your emotions before your emotions take control of you.

EXERCISE 25
Dealing with Disappointment

Many things in your life will not go the way you had hoped or planned. Guaranteed! Some disappointments will be bigger than others, but you can use the following four-step technique to manage how you deal with anything that comes your way. Disappointments will happen, most of them will be out of your control, but you can control how you respond to them by changing how you think to change how you feel.

Step 1

Whenever something doesn't go your way, say to yourself: 'It could be worse'. We know it always could be. This immediately helps you keep a healthy perspective on what has happened, and is a form of gratitude as you are being grateful that whatever happened isn't worse.

Step 2

We know it could always be worse, but now expand that thought outwards and see yourself floating above your life, looking at it from above from start to finish. Has crap happened in the past? Did life go on without much drama? Did you learn from it? As you look down over your entire life you can see that this moment of disappointment was just a redirection that you hadn't expected. It will soon pass, as everything passes.

Step 3

Ask yourself: what am I learning from this? You will be learning something, and by focusing on the lessons, you detract from focusing on the disappointment.

Step 4

Move your body to make your energy flow differently and to change the chemical mix inside you. Jump up and down, punch the air, wave your arms, clap, breathe deeply or whatever movement works for you. If you are in a public place and don't feel comfortable leaping around, just clench your fist discreetly. There are many ways you can move your body, to change the energy flow and to wake up your cells, letting your mind know you are in charge.

If you practise these four steps repeatedly, this simple process will become habitual. You will run over this process unconsciously any time bad things happen. Realising it could be worse, keeping perspective, acknowledging the lessons to be learned, and making a physiological change: these are the four steps to dealing with anything that doesn't go your way.

In summary, you can't control what goes on outside of you, but you can *always control your responses* and your thinking, to control how your energy flows. You can control how you look at life generally. Many of us have evolved with a brain-centric approach to living, but now it's time for a much more heart-centric approach, leading with our hearts not our egos.

Aristotle believed that 'happiness is the meaning and the purpose of life, the whole aim and end of human existence'. Maybe he was partly right; happiness for everyone is a great goal, but the main vehicle of happiness is love. Love is energy, perhaps in its purest life form, and when you focus on giving love, the feeling you get is the energy flow that is most aligned with the ultimate life force flow for you and the universe. When you give love, you first must feel it inside you. Love is a core human need, as you will see in Step 4 , and you are entirely in charge of the love you give, and therefore what you feel.

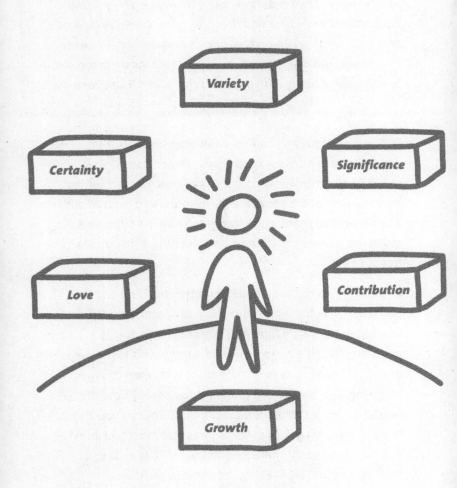

STEP 4

Under-stand Your Human Needs

All human actions are an attempt to meet needs

Marshall Rosenberg

We know from Step 1 that there are over 7 billion individual versions of human alive on Earth today. Each life is a distinct work of art, different but equal, and we think and feel in our own nuanced ways. There are 7 billion versions of reality being experienced right now as a blend of chemicals and life-force energy in each person's body. These forces within cause us to feel how we feel, but we have tools at our disposal to take charge of these forces and manage our thinking and emotion to help us gain the life we want. If we don't take charge we'll simply be passengers reacting to thoughts and feelings as they arise from programming that we didn't design.

Our core human needs

As part of our unique core human operating system we also have in-built needs or drivers, which motivate and guide us to do what we do. These drivers are embedded within us and are part of what it is to be human. They are our *core human needs* and if we cleared out all the programming installed since birth, we would still have these in-built human drivers. We all share these same needs, and we're all trying to meet these needs through our behaviour. What I buy, the way I act, the way I live, all are driven by trying to meet my core human needs.

I am driven to try and meet all these needs but the order in which I prioritise them, and the way in which I try to meet them, will determine my experience of, and degree of fulfilment in, my life. Most people aren't aware of these core needs driving their life as most of the processing is happening unconsciously, but bringing awareness of these needs, and how they shape what you do into your consciousness is one of the most important things you can do to change your life.

As humans, we are above all else programmed to try to stay alive. This survival instinct is a fundamental basic driver which we, and all living creatures, share. Without it, we would be extinct. We all need oxygen, food and water or we will die and we need to be protected from the elements with some form of shelter and security.

Once these needs are met and we have food and feel safe, there are other in-built needs which are part of what makes us human and which we are always striving to meet. Through personal development work we can become more aware of ways to meet these needs that are helpful for the life we want rather than those that block our path to feeling truly fulfilled. We can also learn the importance of prioritising different human needs to cause different outcomes in our experience of life.

Psychologists and academics have long understood there are basic human drivers in all of us, and there have been many theories put forward to describe and explain what these are. If we go back 150 years or so, Charles Darwin was thinking and writing about human drivers, claiming that the most important distinction between us as humans and what he called the 'lower species' is our conscience as a basic evolutionary driving force. Darwin believed humans have endured as a species because we learned to work in groups and rely on problem-solving skills rather than just physical force to help us survive and get what we want. That sense of belongingness or togetherness is also seen as a central need, or human drive.

From theory to action

There are many theories that touch on human needs, but the question to ask is: What can we actually take from these theories to then make a difference in our lives? Understanding may be 'half the job', but only *action* will change your life and take you in the direction you want. This book is about what we can actually do – what action we can take – to make our lives magnificent.

The SYSO System suggests that the easiest way to think about these embedded needs is that there are three types or groups of needs with their nuances and blends being different for each of us. First, we have the need to survive. Second, we have the needs of our personality. Finally, we have needs of our spirit. So, we have Survival, Personality and Spiritual needs. To feel really fulfilled in life, you must meet all three of these needs categories.

When we go deeper into the detail of what each of these needs groups include, it's clear that in different situations and different phases of our life we naturally value different aspects of these needs groups for different reasons. However, in simple terms, presuming you have satisfied your survival needs, it's in meeting your personality and spiritual needs in healthy ways that you will unlock feelings of fulfilment and joy in your life.

It is in these areas of personality and spiritual human needs that the work of Tony Robbins is probably the most useful and practical. Robbins evolved pre-existing theories in presenting his overview of the underlying motivating forces driving the decisions we make in life. Every day we make choices and take actions based on what we think, and Robbins' work invites us to examine the six needs we constantly work to satisfy at a mostly unconscious level. He describes how, through awareness and regular conditioning, we can take charge of these forces in a practical way and work to create the life we want.

Six core needs

In Robbins' theory, we are always trying to meet six core needs as part of our human make-up. These needs influence our deepest motivations and determine how we go about prioritising our decisions and actions. We travel through stages of life where our focus and our priorities may be different, but we all have these six needs that we are always trying to meet through our behaviour. The key is *how* we are trying to meet these needs – whether helpfully or unhelpfully – and how we prioritise them. How we value these six needs and in what order, determines the direction of our life.

> *Whatever emotion you're after, whatever vehicle you pursue – building a business, getting married, raising a family, travelling the world – whatever you think your nirvana is, there are six basic, universal needs that make us tick and drive all human behaviour.*

Tony Robbins

So, let's get familiar with these universal six in-built human needs, and we can then start building the neural networks of understanding and the *action-activating* thoughts to change our behaviour. Understanding and acting in healthy ways to meet these six needs, and the priority in which you meet them, will change your life.

The Need for Certainty

We all have embedded within us the need to feel stable, safe and secure. We need to know, that the sun will rise and that there is oxygen to breathe. We need to feel in control, know we have basic comfort, can avoid pain and to believe there will be some enjoyment in our lives.

Our need for certainty affects how much risk we are willing to take in all areas of our life and the more of a priority and the more extreme we make this, the more we need to feel in control of everything. In some parts of our life, this need for certainty can be very helpful, but in others it is unhelpful.

The world and other people are constantly changing, and so sometimes our need for certainty causes us to build a wall of control around our life, which can mean we stay in our comfort zone and resist change. However, it's important that we don't try to control things that we can't possibly control, as this will lead to immense frustration.

What we can control is how we respond to things. This certainty of being able to *control our response* is how to meet our need for certainty in an empowering and positive way. Creating a sense of centredness, stability and self-belief within us is a positive and healthy way to meet this need. Absolute certainty from within gives the ultimate sense of security in life. The world changes and when we let go of trying to control external factors and trust in the process of life, we understand that one of the main certainties of life is change.

The Need for Variety or Uncertainty

Just as we each need to experience a sense of certainty in the world, it would be pretty boring if we knew everything that was going to happen. 'Variety is the spice of life', as the saying goes, and we all need to feel uncertainty so we can grow as humans. When we step outside our comfort zone we have an opportunity to grow and this interrupts patterns of predictability and stagnation, allowing us to expand and experience more of who we are and who we can be. When we let go of 'needing to know', we enter a realm of possibility that isn't bound by past experience and memories. 'Knowing that we don't know' can be incredibly liberating.

Our efforts to satisfy the need for variety can, however, be taken to extremes if our primary driver is constant change, and we may find ourselves moving homes, changing relationships and searching for new jobs regularly. This constant change can lead to less stability and make it difficult to feel fulfilled. Satisfying the need for variety by constantly changing our external surroundings can prevent us from fully engaging with life right where we are, but *learning and growing* and trying new experiences builds us as humans, enabling us to become more and feel fulfilled by meeting this need in healthy ways.

The Need for Significance

We all want to be seen, to be validated and to feel special for who we are and what we do. The question is how much of a priority in your life is it for you to feel significant and how does this affect your behaviour and how you feel? We don't exist in isolation (more on this in Step 6), but are part of a greater whole. To be an effective part of that whole, we need to know that we're important. Satisfying our need for significance is part of creating our sense of identity and who we are in the world, but the challenge with fulfilling this need is when we become dependent on validation from others in order to feel good about ourselves.

Feeling significant using external means is never going to make you feel fulfilled as this is superficial and you'll be at the mercy of what others think of you. When you stop comparing yourself to others and seeking their approval, instead focusing on getting validation from yourself, your need for significance in unhealthy ways will dissipate.

When we find significance within, we don't need approval from others. An example of significance being fulfilled in a positive way is when we do something that is helpful to others. We feel significant and worthy when we are of service to others. If you feel you have low self-worth, go and do something for someone else. You will have been of worth to them, which will immediately answer your feeling of low self-worth. Giving is a key to a healthy feeling of significance in life and it doesn't have to be material giving. We can give kindness, our time, our listening and our advice, as well as our physical help.

When you lower the priority of needing significance from external factors in your life and instead look to feel *significant from within*, you'll be on a much more powerful and fulfilling path. Spending a lot of money can make you feel significant, and so can spending very little. Some people constantly brag about getting a bargain, or they feel special because they have the most eco-friendly home possible. Some very wealthy people gain significance by hiding their wealth and others by showboating and buying flash cars. This form of significance will ultimately feel hollow.

The Need for Love and Connection

We all have a need to love and be loved by others and to feel connected. This is at the core of our human nature. We're in the womb for around nine months and we're dependent on love as a baby to survive and grow. Love created us and we need other people's love to feel alive.

So it should be no surprise that love and connection with others is central to our experience of fulfilment in life.

> *Love is the oxygen of life; it's what we all want and need most. When we love completely we feel alive, but when we lose love, the pain is so great that most people settle on connection – the crumbs of love.*

Tony Robbins

We can meet this need for love, like all needs, in positive or negative ways. We can get that sense of connection through intimacy, friendship or connecting with ourselves and through empowering self-love, but we can also meet the need for love in a disempowering way by being full of self-pity in a 'poor me' way.

By taking time to genuinely connect with and love the many aspects of ourselves, we can meet this need in a much more helpful way. When we are connected to our self in the truest sense, this connection naturally aligns with and permeates out as a genuine connection and love for others. To give true love you have to feel true love for yourself. The core of most personal development books is this need to love and appreciate yourself first. In Step 1 we looked at how unique and extraordinary we all are. When we love and appreciate ourselves, we're better able to love and appreciate others. To feel love, be that love which you want to feel.

These first four needs – certainty, variety/uncertainty, love/connection and significance – are the four needs of the personality and we all find ways to meet these, but there are two other needs of our spirit. Although not everyone meets these, they are the doorways to our deeper sense of true happiness and ultimate fulfilment in life. Without meeting these in helpful positive ways, our life will always feel like something is missing.

The Need for Growth

For every living thing on Earth to survive and thrive, it must *grow*. The universe is expanding, and life is part of the universe, so growth and expansion of ourselves is essential to be aligned and feel fulfilled. The need for growth both relies on and feeds the first four needs, breathing life into all areas of our existence and as with all our needs, the ways we try and meet this need can be positive or negative for the quality of our life.

For example, growing and expanding can be very fulfilling in its own right, but sometimes striving to fulfil this need obsessively can cause us to limit ourselves from being fully present in life, or to postpone applying our growth and knowledge in the world for fear of not being 'ready' or 'enough'.

However, fulfilling our need for growth comes with an acceptance that *growth is a journey*, not a destination, and that continual growth also means allowing ourselves to be real, to be imperfect and to find authentic ways to share what we discover and learn with others. Growth is a never-ending journey and if you as a person are not growing, you are simply not going to experience real fulfilment in your life.

The Need for Contribution

This is the need to give and to care beyond ourselves. Our need for contribution comes from a fundamental yearning to have our lives mean something, to make a difference, to give or bring something to the world that continues to benefit others when we are gone. Our need for contribution can be fulfilled in many ways, from volunteering, to simply pausing from our busy day to smile, hug or help someone in need.

The challenge with this human need is that once we connect to the power of being of genuine service to the world, we can quite quickly become overwhelmed with all the places, people and animals that are in need of support. Many people who value the need for contribution above all others, also find it difficult to contribute and give to themselves. Contribution, however, comes not only from what we *do*, but from who we are *being*. When we are empowered to meet our need for contribution in the simplest of ways, we are aligned with the universe and we feel fulfilled. Life is really about creating meaning and meaning doesn't come from what you get, it comes from *what you give*.

> *No-one has ever become poor by giving.*

Anne Frank

How are you prioritising your needs?

You should now have a good understanding of the six human needs that are built into all of us. The big practical questions to ask are: how are you prioritising these needs and how are you trying to meet them? Robbins believes your direction in life will largely be determined by which are your top two needs, so let's start by making sure you know which ones they are.

EXERCISE 26
Which Needs Are Your Priority?

Now you understand about human needs and how they drive us to do the things we do, which needs do you think have been the main drivers for you in your life until now?

Write along the top of a piece of paper the top six human needs that we all have within us:

Certainty—Variety—Significance—Connection—Growth—Contribution

Underneath this list, draw a vertical line down the middle to split the rest of the page in two.

On the left-hand side of the line, write down the order in which you think you have been prioritising meeting your needs. There is no right or wrong answer in this exercise; the only thing that matters is that you are honest with yourself. It's your life, and honesty is the fastest way to making a better life. It doesn't have to be exact and you may find your priorities change in different circumstances.

When you have done this, circle the top two needs on your list.

Remember, you're trying to meet all six of your needs so don't get too weighed down interrogating your list. It's likely you'll know instinctively which two have been your priority needs anyway.

Now on the right-hand side of the page, create your new list of priorities and circle the new top two needs, which you're going to prioritise in the future.

Robbins believes focusing on the top two needs explains a lot about the choices we make in life. In society today, significance and certainty tend to be reinforced as the most important needs and it's no surprise that these are often the top two needs for most people. Look at your needs and the top two you have identified. Ask yourself how having these at the top has affected the choices you have made in your life so far. By being more aware, you can decide to change your top two needs so you can travel in a new, more fulfilling direction in life. It's not always easy to change quickly because your needs system is deeply programmed, but by starting with awareness you are making the first critical step.

> ☞ *Having your top needs as growth and contribution will give you the greatest sense of fulfilment in life.*

Contribution is really a form of love, and connecting with others and feeding your spirit will make you feel fulfilled in ways that trying to be certain or significant never will.

Look at those around you; it's likely that the most genuinely happy people you know have *love, growth and contribution* as their top needs, and the least happy usually have significance and certainty as their top two needs. The good news is you can make a change in the priority of your needs anytime once you're aware, and you can practice and reinforce this change until it becomes habitual.

How are you meeting your needs?

When you understand that your top needs are heavily responsible for shaping your life, the next step is to be aware of how you are meeting them and whether this is empowering and enhancing your life, or whether you are sabotaging yourself. Meeting your needs in healthy ways is a critical part of the system for creating an outstanding life.

> *Everyone experiences the same six human needs. However, everyone finds different ways of satisfying these needs. Each of these needs can be met in ways that are positive or negative. Some ways of satisfying these needs are good for the person, good for others, and good for society, and some are bad for everyone.*

Cloé Madanes

EXERCISE 27
How Have You Been Meeting Your Needs?

On a clean sheet of paper, write down the ways you believe you have been meeting each need, based on your list from the last exercise.

For example, to meet the need for significance you might have been buying things in the hope others will think of you in a certain way.

Write down anything that comes into your mind about each need and your behaviour in meeting that need.

The purpose is not to have an exhaustive list, but to stimulate your thinking and awareness in this area so you can start to make more effective choices of ways you can meet these needs.

Meeting your need for significance by looking for validation from others and meeting your need for certainty by trying to control everything won't make you happy. If you're trying to look good all the time for others you'll feel an emptiness inside. If you are constantly comparing yourself to others there are always going to be people who have more or are 'better' than you against whatever criteria you are measuring. And it's impossible to always have certainty, as life is uncertain. The only certainty is the certainty you bring from *within* you.

In Step 5 , we will look at the importance of having a clear sense of purpose for your life, and you'll see how this can link in many ways to contribution, growth and love.

If you meet three or more of your human needs with a particular way of behaving then that behaviour is likely to become addictive, so we need to make really sure that we're meeting our needs in positive ways.

One of the biggest ways to sabotage yourself in your life is through self-pity. Pitying yourself is not helpful. There are more *empowering* ways to look at everything that happens in your life. We discussed how taking responsibility for your life experience is critical and that, while we can't control much of what happens, we can always control the meanings we give to what is happening to us.

However, the reason self-pity can become an emotional home that is frequented by many people is that it simply meets some of your human needs, and usually at least three. It can make you feel significant to have 'problems'; you can connect with yourself, and this kind of thinking can give you certainty as you know the feeling well. The challenge is to become aware of what is happening, and to see that the way you are meeting your needs is unhelpful. Try and meet your need for significance, for example, by being a positive force in the world, and meet your need for certainty from your inner strength and knowledge that you can always control your response.

> *I think everybody should get rich and famous and do everything they ever dreamed of so they can see that it's not the answer.*

Jim Carrey

Achievement and fulfilment

In society, we're generally encouraged to be achievers and achievement is seen as the high marker of success. We celebrate people who we identify as having made great achievements. This is commendable in many ways and plays a huge part in society and for the individual, but 'achievement' and 'fulfilment' are very different. Most of us are striving for achievements in our life. We have goals for our career, our finances, and the possessions we want, and achievement in this sense is just a science. It follows certain steps and if we apply the steps, we'll increase the probability of 'achieving'. However, for all the achieving and all the progress we have made as human beings, we seem to be unhappier than ever. Statistics on depression and unhappiness show no precise link between happiness and money or material achievement, and we regularly hear about the high-flying career executive, business person or celebrity who seemingly has everything they wanted to achieve, but who is deeply unhappy and 'depressed'.

 What you get will never make you sustainably happy and fulfilled. What you become will.

And at the heart of 'becoming more' is understanding our human needs and how we are meeting them.

Achievement is a science, whereas *fulfilment is an art*, but we aren't taught about this art. The art lies in understanding the keys to fulfilment, and rather than seeking to have more, we should realise that it is richer to 'be more'. The world is full of many achievers who are miserable and it's the feeling of being fulfilled, of feeling really alive and full of joy, that is to be really successful, yet we focus our teaching mainly around the science of achievement. However, by following the SYSO System you can commit to making the most of your life, having an experience of both achievement and fulfilment and in full knowledge that they are not mutually exclusive. In fact, they can be mutually reinforcing.

Seeking deeper fulfilment in your life rather than short-term unsustainable pleasure boosts, having a purpose bigger than yourself and focusing on growing and giving, will transform your experience. This is indeed the secret to living.

EXERCISE 28
Review Your Needs

Make an audit before you go to sleep of some of the things you did today and which needs they met.

For example, how much of what you did today was because of what you wanted others to think of you? Be completely honest. That is how you will make the greatest changes to your experience of life.

You can make notes as a checklist or just work through it in your mind. The important thing is to become more aware of your needs, and how you are prioritising and meeting them.

Find a way of remembering the six needs. Write them down, make notes on your phone or whatever you need to help remember these innate human needs you have of certainty, variety, significance, connection, growth and contribution.

STEP 5

Be Clear About the Purpose of Your Life

The best way to find yourself is to lose yourself in the service of others.

Mahatma Gandhi

There are things about life which it seems wise to accept that we cannot understand while we are alive. Letting go and being comfortable with this uncertainty can be liberating, lightening and can dramatically increase the quality of our lives. Knowing we don't know invites us to trust in life, trust in that which created you, whatever you believe 'that' to be. It is stressful always to need to be certain about your life and in control, and it's also not that attractive for those around you if you're uptight, controlling and craving certainty. Let go. Breathe deeply. Smile. Feel your aliveness and simply appreciate being.

Our only real certainty is what happens at the end of being alive, which for everyone, of course, is death. Although we don't know what happens after our life is over, we do know that life was here long before we were born and life is likely to go on long after we die.

Our place in time

So, if life is not just about you or me or any individual life, what does it all mean? What is the *purpose of* us being here, especially when we consider that our time here is for such a relatively very short period in comparison to all of life time?

> *Time is long, but life is short.*

> Stevie Wonder

☞ *Think about how much life has gone before us, and that seems likely will follow us, and keep in perspective how your life is a small, but essential, part of all life.*

We are dependent on the past, we influence the future and without individual life, there is no collective life. Every expression of life is an essential part of the whole. We are all VIPs and everything we do affects more than just us.

Our home, Earth, is thought to be a little over 4.5 billion years old, and life itself is believed to have originated here around 3.8 billion years ago from tiny individual cells of bacteria. About 2.8 billion years ago, there were multicellular forms of life and only in the last 570 million years did the kinds of life forms we're familiar with begin to evolve. Mammals are thought not to have existed until about 200 million years ago and we as humans, or *Homo sapiens*, are only about 200,000 years old.

And this is just looking at the time that has passed. The more time that passes in the future, the more of a small flicker our life will have been.

Your unique contribution

Life goes on but the individual does not, and life, therefore, is not all about us. It is *about* us but not *all* about us. There is so much more than just our life. Rather than feeling that our individual lives are therefore relatively insignificant, we should instead appreciate that we have a critical role, a huge potential, to make an *infinite* contribution to the greater whole, which we are all a part of. The whole is only the whole because of the parts, because of each of us. Without an awareness of this bigger picture and without a clear philosophy for our purpose here, it could easily feel like it doesn't matter how we live as we'll soon be gone. However, when we understand that all of life is interconnected (Step 6) and that we have an impact that goes far beyond each of us infinitely, we can become acutely aware that every life is absolutely critical in the role it plays to the whole of life.

When we understand the contribution our life makes to the whole of life, and when we have a clear philosophy about the purpose of our life, we can feel liberated, valuable and comfortable with uncertainty.

We will also feel most content when we are being the best version of the person we are capable of being. For example, if we were designed to be a light then it would be our shining and illuminating that would make us feel useful and content, doing that which we were designed to do as best we can. Our experience would be optimised and we would be at our most valuable.

Life is about you and lighting yourself up, but it is also about your impact and how you can *illuminate* other life. Changing your perspective in this way will change your life and we should remind ourselves what a special gift it is to be alive, but also a responsibility, for ourselves and for other life.

The 'wow' of the everyday

Living is a special occasion and should call for regular celebration. Most people feel a sense of 'wow' when they see a beautiful sunset or a full moon, but what if we felt this sense of 'wow' about everyday things in life too? When we orientate ourselves to feeling 'wow' at the sight of a tree, at a bird singing, the touch of water running over our hands, the taste of our favourite fruit, or the smell of a beautiful flower, when we start to appreciate the beauty and wonder all around us, we can start to feel even more grateful that we are here now as something miraculous and amazing, and as part of the whole.

Without this sense of perspective and without understanding our purpose and direction, how can we know what to do with our life? What direction to take? How do we evaluate how well we are living? Having a clear philosophy about the purpose of your life, understanding you are here to enjoy yourself *and* contribute to life, will instead give you the biggest source of strength, certainty and feeling of aliveness.

If you get into your car, but don't know why or where you are going, then you're probably going to feel frustrated and lost. In life, unfortunately, many people feel frustrated and lost because they simply lack clarity about where they are going and why they are going there, or the purpose of their life. Most people just 'idle' on their programmed beliefs, seeking pleasure and avoiding pain, but without a clear sense of purpose, life can feel hollow and like something is missing.

When we are living without realising our potential to benefit life beyond ourselves, we will probably feel an emptiness. It can also be quite scary as death approaches if you don't have a *philosophy* that includes the greater sense of your life as an essential part of all life. If the ultimate source of anxiety is fear of and uncertainty about the future, we know for sure that the future ends in death for each of us in the form we are now. Death is the only certainty.

Facing up to death

Facing up to death, accepting its inevitability, and integrating it into a life philosophy that starts with how useful we are to other lives while we are here will help us make the most of the gift of our time alive. As humans, we have the capacity to think consciously, and to ask questions about death and why we are here. This could be what separates humans from other forms of life.

Purpose of any kind gives us focus and helps us feel alive. Finding your purpose has long been central to most personal development approaches. There are numerous books on this topic alone. Religious texts, such as the Bible, for example, are often thought of as the first and most significant teachings on meaning and purpose in life, but there has been much theorising about human purpose since life began, and many interpretations have emerged over the years.

The key question is really how can we use any theory in terms of *practical* application to our own living experience? Some theories suggest we sacrifice our own pleasure for the pursuit of others and yet some propose living life just for yourself.

Be a beacon of happiness

The SYSO System suggests focusing on enjoying yourself *and* on being the best contributor you can. These are actually both mutually reinforcing, because by pursuing a life of contribution you will get feelings of happiness and joy from that. When you feel really happy and full of joy in your life, you are likely to be the best contributor to other lives.

Perhaps the best way to think about how to reach your fullest potential for fulfilment is to think of yourself as being a beacon of happiness, rather than a receiver of happiness.

> *This is the true joy in life, the being used for a purpose recognised by yourself as a mighty one; the being thoroughly worn out before you are thrown on the scrap heap; the being a force of nature instead of a feverish selfish little clod of ailments and grievances complaining that the world will not devote itself to making you happy.*
>
> *George Bernard Shaw*

Many self-improvement books talk about finding our unique purpose, or the special 'something' that we are born to do with our lives. However, instead of thinking about finding a unique purpose for ourselves, it can be more helpful to focus on the main purpose we all have, the bigger purpose, of all human life. Once we clearly understand that *bigger picture* there are many ways we can live a fulfilling life within that vision. Apart from also putting much less pressure on ourselves to find the 'one special thing we were born to do', we can stay open to creating the life we want by thinking about the many passions and purposes we might have, rather than concentrating on having just one.

However, the big question: 'What is the purpose of human life?' can seem overwhelming.

Religion has long been the main guide for many, with narratives, symbols and traditions that are intended to give meaning to life. According to some estimates, there are around 4,200 religions in the world and nearly 75% of the world's population practices one of the five most influential religions: Buddhism, Christianity, Hinduism, Islam or Judaism. Christianity and Islam together are estimated to cover the religious affiliation of more than half of the world's population. Over 80% of all living humans subscribe to beliefs in the form of organised religious belief systems, and while the number of religiously unaffiliated people has grown globally, many of these 'non-believers' still have some form of religious-type beliefs based on their cultural programming. Organised religion is humanity's biggest programming machine and has been our biggest source of theory on meaning and purpose, but it has also been the cause of much conflict and confusion.

Some religious doctrines suggest that our purpose is to find happiness, to love others, to become the best version of ourselves, to follow God's will, or all of these, and there is great merit in many of these theories. However, it seems there often isn't real clarity about our purpose in the highest, simplest, purest sense.

With the SYSO System, which is concerned with practical applications, there is a much simpler way to look at this question without it being a cumbersome topic to dance around or avoid. Your clear philosophy on the purpose of your life should be your compass for everything, for the direction you take in your life and against which you can evaluate your time here.

If you work for a successful business, for example, you'll no doubt clearly know the purpose of the business, which is usually to make money by selling products or services. If you join a gym, you'll have a clear purpose for doing that, and if you choose to book a holiday, you have a clear purpose about why and where you would like to go. Our life is no different; we need to have a clear purpose about what we are doing here or there will always be a confusing void in our life.

If everything is just about us, life won't be fulfilling, and that's not why we are here. If it's always about others, with no *joy* for ourselves, it will seem unbalanced and we won't be realising the gift of our human experience.

So, in simple terms, it's about both. It's about being happy and contributing to something beyond ourselves. These are mutually reinforcing and the highest purpose of all life is to be *useful* to, and *supporting of*, other life.

'Usefulment'

The SYSO System suggests a new word to describe the target for a happy and fulfilled life. This word is 'usefulment', which is the feeling of fulfilment we experience by feeling our life is of use. We have already said life isn't just about each of us, and by being useful we're not acting just for ourselves. But we've also said life is about you and we shouldn't think of being useful and being happy as two separate things.

 The purpose of life is to enjoy and make the most of your own life while being useful and making the most impact on other life.

The key point of this chapter is that life goes on and we in our human form do not , and so the impact of our life should be measured in terms of the impact on other life. It has to be about more than just living for yourself, and if you look for evidence of the most fulfilled and sustainably happy people, you will likely notice a trend; they tend to be orientated towards what they can do for others. About 80 years of living, if we are fortunate, is a 'long time' in many ways to be alive, and we can experience so much in that length of time, but our own living has to be about more than just the time we are alive. Everything is more than the individual part and we are all more than our individual life. We are all *interconnected* (Step 6).

> *Inter-dependence, of course, is a fundamental law of nature. Not only higher forms of life but also many of the smallest insects are social beings who, without any religion, law or education, survive by mutual cooperation based on an innate recognition of their interconnectedness.*

The Dalai Lama

We were created because of events prior to our own birth, which happened because of events prior to those, and events prior to those, and so on. We have an effect that carries on long after our time alive on Earth through the *impact* we have on others, who have impact on others, and so on.

 Our life is about much more than just our time alive; it's about something bigger than ourselves.

When we start to tune into and build deep awareness from that perspective, we orientate ourselves to the impact our life can have on other lives and in doing so, we will feel much more fulfilled, aligned and deeply grounded.

Your life purpose

In the SYSO System, the purpose of life is the impact we can make on other lives while at the same time enjoying our own life. That's it. Your life purpose isn't more complicated than that and shouldn't be a heavy load for you to overthink or try and figure out. How you live in heading towards that overriding objective is now up to you, to create a life in line with what you enjoy and what you can do that is useful.

> *When I went to school, they asked me what I wanted to be when I grew up. I wrote down happy. They told me I didn't understand the assignment. I told them they didn't understand life.*

John Lennon

If you're spending your life doing things you don't enjoy and not making a contribution to life, you will probably feel something is missing and that you're not fully alive. Think about enjoying life and contributing to other life, not either/or. Contributing to life beyond ourselves provides a great sense of enjoyment or fulfilment, and the more we are enjoying life, the more likely we are to be the best contributor and help make others feel good. It is mutually reinforcing, like the pattern of all life.

Helping others may just be the secret to living a life that is not only *happier but also healthier*. Giving releases endorphins in much the same way that exercise does and the 'rush' that people sometimes experience after performing an altruistic act has been referred to as 'helper's high'.

Growing and giving

Now we have a clear articulation and philosophy for what our life is about, we can measure the success of living in terms of the impact we have on other lives, and the enjoyment we have while affecting other lives. Growing and giving is the secret to living, and focusing on this mantra will lead us on a path to deeper fulfilment in life.

Achieving is really a science, or a series of steps to follow, whereas fulfilment, as we looked at in Step 4, can be considered much more of an art. We now have the 'how' of this art, by focusing on a life of 'usefulment'. Generally, when you ask people what the meaning and purpose of their life is, their answers will be complex, but it isn't really that complicated. Enjoy yourself and help others. That's all you need to focus on. That is your purpose.

> *If you want happiness for an hour, take a nap. If you want happiness for a day, go fishing. If you want happiness for a year, inherit a fortune. If you want happiness for a lifetime, help somebody.*

Chinese proverb

Some might ask themselves, 'Once I focus on the contribution my life can have on other lives, what is the purpose above that? Why does life exist at all?' But what if you let go of that question and instead accept that you aren't going to get an answer in this lifetime? Give it up to that which created you and *trust in the process*. Focus on the purpose of being useful to life and the feeling that gives you.

If you're still not convinced, think about what alternative philosophies you could have, such as just living for yourself, a winner-takes-all attitude, or a belief that everything is a battle and screw everyone else. Or at the other extreme, giving everything to others without considering yourself at all. In all these philosophies, you are going to be unfulfilled. The first three approaches will leave you spiritually empty and the other one will leave you exhausted and just as empty because you'll have failed to look after yourself.

Practise living a life where you know that everything you do goes beyond you. Realise the value you can have impacting other lives.

☞ *Everything you do is important.*

Commit today, if you haven't already, to your new simple and clear philosophy about life, which will guide you in everything you do. Think about the ripple effect of all your actions and make sure you're crystal clear about this new, clearly defined purpose. Write it down, put it on a Post-it note and keep checking in against this to assess how you are doing. Ask if what you are doing at any time is aligned with your purpose. Ask yourself how you can have more fun and more positive impact on others. With a clear direction, you should feel amazing – growing and experiencing the secret of joyful living.

EXERCISE 29
Know Your Purpose

Write down your purpose:

'My purpose is to enjoy life and help others.'

Say it really clearly.

Say it loudly and repeatedly, as an affirmation.

Check in with yourself at the end of every day for 30 days. Score yourself on a scale of 1 to 10 on how you lived that day in alignment with your purpose.

Ask yourself your two purpose questions:

Am I enjoying myself?

Am I contributing?

Celebrate your giving and become more aware of the gift of the feeling that is giving.

Stick a copy of your written purpose, your life slogan, where you can see it – on your computer as your screensaver, on your dashboard, on a mirror.

This is your 'satnav destination' and the journey will be amazing!

'My purpose is to enjoy life and help others.'

Once you take the focus of your life away from it being just about you to being about you so you can be about others, you'll feel different. You'll radiate calm and contentment. People will experience you differently and sense your certainty in life. You will be your most self-assured and it will show, radiating out from you as an authentic human being.

Most emotional problems are because we're focused too much on ourselves. Keep remembering that life isn't just about you. It is about all of us. We are all in the same boat, and others aren't your enemy, even if it might seem like that sometimes. Keep it light and see life through the lens of fun and giving. We are a small but incredibly important part of the tree of life, and we are all related. Perhaps a better way to look at life is thinking about how you can look after others, your brothers and sisters on the same journey.

> *It is because our own human existence is so dependent on the help of others that our need for love lies at the very foundation of our existence. Therefore, we need a genuine sense of responsibility and a sincere concern for the welfare of others.*

Dalai Lama

EXERCISE 30
Highlight Your Purpose on Your Vision Board

In Step 2 you created your own personal vision board of the life you want. Revisit this board now and write your purpose in big bold letters:

'MY PURPOSE IS TO ENJOY LIFE AND HELP OTHERS.'

This is the most important part of your vision board as it sets your overall direction. You can look at all the aspects of the vision you created and ask yourself: 'Are there any changes I need to make, or does everything align perfectly with my new clarity on what my life is about?'

Give your smile

Now you have more *clarity about your purpose* you will become more consciously aware of how you are living and the impact it has far beyond just yourself. There is a ripple effect in every action and interaction, and in everything you do, say or think. Recognise your power and take responsibility for being a happy soul. Be kind, judge others

by their intentions and realise not everyone has evolved
or become conscious to the level you have. Life is for living.
By giving you will feel most alive, and there is one thing you
can give easily, anytime, and for free; your smile. Give your
smile and see how it feels for you and everyone you give it to.
When you see someone without a smile, give them yours.

Death is not the end

My father died suddenly and unexpectedly on the second
green while playing golf on the 6 July 2009 at 9.34 a.m.
A cardiac arrest didn't give him much chance of survival
given where he was, at a time when defibrillators were much
less common. It was a shock and sad, but I remember two
things vividly when I attended the hospital that afternoon
with my mother and sisters to identify his body. First, he was
still there, in physical form, but it was immediately clear that
the life force had gone from his body. As I cried, my tears and
energy in motion were initially from the realisation his life
had passed and thoughts of missing him terribly. But then
in a second, intense realisation, my thoughts turned to
how many others his life had touched and I felt a calmness
knowing his life hadn't just disappeared. It lives on and in
everything he touched. It lives on through the impact he
had on others and the impact they had on others, and so on.

No one knows what happens when we die, but we do know
our bodies are still here after the *life energy* force has gone.
This energy has left your earthly body form, but it is still

in the universe; there is nowhere else for it to go. All the impacts you have had on other lives live on; there is nowhere else for them to go, and they live on in the lives of everyone you touched and the lives of everyone they have touched. When you become more aware of this, you understand and act differently, knowing your life is much more than just the time you are alive on Earth.

EXERCISE 31
Be a Beacon of 'Usefulment' and Joy

For the next three days, focus on consciously being a beacon of 'usefulment' and joy to everyone you come into contact with. Everyone from a shop assistant to your friends, family and co-workers.

Think of yourself as a vessel whose purpose is to be of use to life around you.

Smile at strangers and be natural and warm and open – without being creepy!

Each evening, informally review your thoughts:

How did being a beacon of 'usefulment' and joy make you feel?

How do you think it made others feel?

How do you think it changed the interactions you had?

> *Imagine the ripple effect of how you were with others and how they may then have been with people they interacted with.*
>
> *Did you enjoy doing that and did you feel useful?*

For some people, this may be a more dramatic change of approach than for others, but the purpose is to become more aware of the impact your orientation can have, and your own feelings. Of course, you cannot control how others react to you being a *beacon of 'usefulment'* and joy, but it would only be those who are not happy themselves who would be anything other than welcoming and warmed by such a giving orientation.

By having a clear, simple and easy-to-follow philosophy for the purpose of your life you have a filter through which you can ask the same question of anything: 'Does this fit with my purpose?' As this check becomes habitual, you'll feel life flowing naturally and you will love your journey, by enjoying yourself and knowing you're having a really meaningful impact on other lives as you keep growing.

> *The sole meaning of life is to serve humanity.*
>
> *Leo Tolstoy*

Appre-ciate Your Intercon-nected-ness

Learn how to see. Realise that everything is connected to everything else.

Leonardo da Vinci

There are more people alive today than ever before and there are more and easier ways for everyone to connect because of advances in technology and transport. Most of us are also living closer to each other, yet people report themselves as feeling more apart.

Both the UK and US governments have declared loneliness as a big public health issue that affects all ages, not just older people living on their own. In the UK, a recent study described loneliness as an epidemic, claiming that 9 million people always or often feel lonely, and that a third of men admitted to feeling lonely at least once a week. Despite the growing population, the advancements in communication technology and the connective power of social media, the experience of loneliness seems to have never been more prevalent.

Say goodbye to loneliness

Seeing ourselves as separate is actually at the heart of most of our social problems. We are clearly less alone in the world than ever but when we think we're more alone, we're programming ourselves to feel unhappy. If the world was a room, it's filling up, and the more people there are in the room, the more possibilities there are for interacting.

This thing we call 'being lonely' usually tends to be described as something beyond our control. The SYSO

System disagrees. Of course, we don't want people to feel lonely, but the responsibility lies with each of us. Implying it is someone else's problem than our own to fix takes away the individual's responsibility and the power we have over how we experience our life.

In Stockholm, six out of ten households have just one occupant, yet Swedes are less likely than the average European to complain of loneliness. 'Being' lonely can be more accurately described as 'doing' lonely and for most people, it is a choice. The solution is very simple; change how you think and you can stop 'doing' lonely thinking.

 Wake up to the important role you have in all life, the depth of your being, and the value you can add to other lives.

The way to start not feeling lonely and to change the pattern of 'I'm lonely' thinking is to understand how important your *contribution is to the whole*. Understanding the interconnectedness of life and our role in this system changes the focus away from thinking about what we're getting from life, to how we can be a source of use and love to others. When we do that, we can spread good in the world rather than feeling sorry for ourselves by imagining that we're alone. We are never alone; there are more than 7 billion of us here!

The key to self-worth

If someone is 'doing' lonely thinking by questioning their self-worth, which stops them choosing to interact with others, the best way to change that feeling is for them to *do something for others*. They would then instantly feel they are being of use and have worth. Your ultimate self-worth comes from your worth to life and this self-worth is pre-programmed; it is already within you.

If you feel lonely then the first thing to do is reach out to connect with others in a giving way.

 Kindness, fun and compassion are always in demand, and if that's your focus you will never feel alone; you will feel useful and others will want to be with you.

If you feel lonely, talk to someone: smile at them, compliment them, tell them how much they mean to you, write to them, send them a photo, make something for them, remind them how important they are to you, inquire about them, be interested, or remind them of a great memory of a time you shared.

Our source is love

We exist because of others. We exist because of love from something other than ourselves. We exist because of the life energy we have within us, which must have come from somewhere – it must have come from a source, and this source is always there. Every day we should be grateful to that which gave us life. Every day we should be grateful for our source which is always there. *May the source be with you!* If you are struggling to feel this love that is always in you, focus instead on giving it. When you give love, you will feel love.

We might physically be alone at times, but we always have a choice whether to think lonely thoughts or not. Of course, because of health or mobility limitations, some people may have less physical interaction with other people. Others are financially restricted, but with the internet and mobile phones, almost everyone can communicate with other people and they can communicate to be a source of goodness to others. If you want more or better friendships, start with giving friendship or being a better friend.

 Give that which you want to receive is a fundamental principle of life.

EXERCISE 32
Pour Your Love and Kindness

For one week, pick a chunk of time each day when you have an opportunity to interact with others. It could be an hour or two depending on where you are and what you are doing. The exact length of time isn't important.

Decide for that period of time each day just to focus on how much love and kindness you can give. It could be giving in person, by letter, or with a phone call, but the idea is to focus as much as possible on giving the gifts of love and kindness.

Don't worry if you slip out of awareness now and again, just try and focus in every situation and interaction on pouring out love and kindness.

At the end of the week review how it felt:

Did it feel easy to be orientated that way?

Did others react to you differently?

Did it feel good?

You can do this exercise anytime. It is more of an ongoing conditioning regime than a specific exercise, and making this orientation habitual and part of your identity will magnify the quality of your life experience.

All life is connected

We can choose to think about ourselves as a tiny, seemingly inconsequential grain of sand in the whole scheme of life and, because we are not physically attached to anyone or anything, we're on our own in a vast universe. Many people think like this, believing their life is finite and that they are separate from everything else. However, this type of programming and thinking about separateness and life's end isn't going to make us feel great. Instead, the key to appreciating the greater depth and expanse of our being lies in understanding that all life is connected. By appreciating the *interconnectedness of everything* we'll realise how the concept of loneliness is actually ridiculous.

> *You are never alone. You are eternally connected with everyone.*

Amit Ray

Thinking about how you are interconnected with the world and having a clear philosophy for the important purpose of your life (Step 5) is the key to never feeling lonely. You are part of life and you don't just exist for yourself. You will be physically alone at times, but you are never really alone in the world. Alone and lonely are very different. Being on your own isn't lonely and there are many examples of people who choose to spend a great deal of time without others being physically present. Buddhist monks choose to be alone for extraordinary amounts of time and yet they don't feel lonely. They experience regular solitude, but they feel completely connected because Buddhism at its core is based on the concept that everything is one.

Let's be clear. We all have pain to deal with in various ways and at various stages of our life. One of our important human needs is to feel connection with others, and for some people there is physical isolation on top of physical illness. This book is about *helping people help themselves* and how everyone can make themselves feel better deliberately. How we choose to think about ourselves and in relation to others affects how we feel, and therefore affects the quality of our life.

My mother, who is in her eighties, talks to a friend of a similar age regularly on the phone and says her friend often talks about feeling lonely. She complains that nobody has been to see her, no-one has called or written for a while. My mother asked her, 'Have you been out today?' 'No.' 'Have you called anyone?' 'No.' 'Have you written to anyone?' 'No.' All those actions were possible for her, but she chose instead to think of being lonely as something she wasn't in control of, and in thinking like that, she didn't take responsibility for how she wanted to feel. Friendship and connection are available to her and to everyone all the time if we start by giving, or being the friend we would like others to be.

This chapter is about interconnectedness and so you may wonder why it has started with so much about loneliness. By examining how our thinking determines feelings of loneliness we can appreciate how being aware of our interconnectedness, and our role in life, can change how we are feeling and therefore how we behave. We are all interconnected. And how we think about our place in life is going to determine how we feel. We might feel inconsequential at times, but as soon as we start becoming more aware that we're an integral part of something much bigger, we change our perspective on our living experience.

EXERCISE 33
Do Less Lonely

How lonely would you say you are?

Give yourself an intuitive loneliness score for your current life, out of 10. Don't overthink it, just give a number and write this down.

What percentage roughly of your life would you say you feel lonely to some degree? Again, write this down.

Now over the next few days commit to doing the following:

Talk to three new people each day. This can be anyone – a shop assistant, your bus or train driver or a neighbour. Ask them questions – it can be a short conversation, but it must be a conversation. Be interested in their answers and their life.

Smile at others. If you are used to keeping your head down or avoiding eye contact, this may seem a creepy exercise to you. Do it anyway; you'll probably benefit the most!

Give five compliments each day. Make them genuine. It could be as simple as saying something like 'Thank you, that service was fantastic, you're great' to waiting staff, or 'I saw how kind you were to that person, it was really lovely' when you witness a kind act.

Each day contact someone you haven't heard from for a while. With all the technology available, this is easy. It could be a text message, an email or a phone call. Remind yourself to give friendship if you want to receive it.

Make a conscious decision to visit an elderly person or care home in the next ten days. Ask questions, listen, and help people polish some of their memories.

There are so many other things you could do, but do these five things as a start for a few days and then revisit your score. How lonely do you now feel on a scale of 1 to 10 and for what percentage of your life do you feel lonely?

Everything exists to serve something more than itself

In looking at how everything in life is interconnected, let's start with thinking about the actual bodies that we live in. No part of our body exists in isolation or just for itself; it all has a purpose to serve something more than itself. This is a fundamental principle in life. Everything in life has a role to play, a purpose, an important part that is more than just itself. We all exist to serve something more than our self and all of life exists to support some other form of life.

The human body is made up of about 37 trillion cells and each on its own could easily seem completely inconsequential as such a tiny part of the whole, but they all work together and we only exist as a collection of all of them. Think of any part of your body. The heart, for example doesn't exist just for the heart, the liver doesn't just exist for the liver. *Every part of us has a role to play in a bigger part.* Everything is connected and interdependent.

Blaming the past

One of the common sources of unhelpful, unhappy thinking is when we look at our life and wish things hadn't happened the way they did. We blame our past, we blame people, and we make excuses for how our life is now because of this.

☞ *Everyone has crap in their past, but what if it was supposed to play out the way it did? What if it was working for you, and for all life?*

No matter what has happened, be *grateful* for what your past has given you, the lessons you've learnt, and have faith in the process and what lies ahead.

EXERCISE 34
Blame Your Past Effectively

Think of something in your life that, when it happened, you thought it was terrible at the time. Perhaps you were betrayed or you lost something that was really important to you.

Now ask yourself what positive things have happened as a result of that 'bad' event.

Did a relationship break-up lead you to meet someone amazing you would not have otherwise met? Did it cause you to take a change of direction in your life? Who did you meet? What did you do that would not have otherwise happened?

If you are going to blame your past, make sure you also blame it for all the positive effects too, and be thankful for all the lessons you have learnt.

There is usually gold in what you think are your problems, and adversity can be your greatest teacher.

The wound is where the light enters you.

Rumi

Chain of events

We are all closer to each other than we might think; you may have heard of the 'six degrees of separation' theory, which suggests that every human on the planet is six or fewer social connections away from each other. In this sense, the world is smaller than we may imagine. If we start appreciating how we are all connected, all related and that everyone is just trying to do their best with what they have and where they are – even though their brain processing and programming have evolved differently – then we are likely to be more understanding and see more good in the world.

Being interconnected is part of being human and we know from Step 4 that we all have the need to feel connection with others.

EXERCISE 35
The Chain of Events

Sit comfortably for a few moments and just let your thoughts flow, thinking about people who might have been involved in making the things around you: your clothes, your furniture, your home, your car, and the food you are eating, for example.

Think of the chain of events that happened for each item. The number of people who would have been involved in design, development, production, distribution and selling.

Nothing is around you without a chain of prior events and people involved in those. Even if you made your own clothes or built your own house, you needed other people, and those people needed other people, who needed others and so on.

As you think about this, you'll become more aware of the interconnectedness of everything and that will help

Life supports other life

All living things are connected to each other, because *each organism depends on others* for support. In order to thrive, plants get energy from the sun. We, as humans, receive the by-product from plants, which is oxygen. Animals eat plants, while other animals eat them, and on it goes in the food chain, with multiple branches being a great web of all life.

Think of trees. They breathe in carbon dioxide and breathe out oxygen. Humans need to inhale oxygen and breathe out carbon dioxide. Trees and humans support each other's growth. Trees, like other green plants, use photosynthesis to convert the carbon dioxide into sugar, cellulose and carbohydrates, which that they use for food and growth. Trees also absorb other potentially harmful gases, such as sulphur dioxide and carbon monoxide from the air and they release oxygen. One large tree can provide a day's supply of oxygen for four people. If we reduce the number of trees, we affect much more than just the trees.

Here is a floating cloud in this sheet of paper. Without a cloud, there will be no rain; without the rain, the trees cannot grow; and without trees, we cannot make paper. If the cloud is not here, the sheet of paper cannot be here either.

Thich Nhat Hanh

Everything is connected to its environment since its existence depends on the conditions of the *environment*. The same life force is within all of us albeit in its own unique form, and every living expression has a role to play in the ecosystem. Life supports other life. Nothing exists on its own and even though we appear unconnected physically, we are interconnected in invisible ways in the whole system of life, and through air, light, food and energy.

We are all distantly related

There is plenty of evidence to show that all of life's species are related and that we're all descended from a common ancestor. Charles Darwin reported evidence of these relationships over 150 years ago and he highlighted obvious anatomical similarities between both living and extinct diverse species. With his 1859 book, *On the Origin of Species by Means of Natural Selection*, Darwin not only explained the diversity of life around us but he also showed how all life is connected.

More recent research has focused on showing how all organisms are related genetically and these relationships can be represented in an evolutionary tree, known as the Tree of Life. We know now that most of what we consider to be resemblances are expressions of our *shared genetic coding*, which is the direct outcome of a common ancestry. If you have ever thought someone looks like a dog or a goat for example, you might be right, as it could well be a very real likeness because of this shared ancestry!

There has been an enormous amount of research in this area and we're learning much more about how we are all individually, biologically coded from a blend of genetic coding before us. There is still much to learn, but one thing is for sure, we're all distantly related. Darwin was the first person to present this idea and he showed how any two things share a common ancestor at some point in the past.

The Tree of Life

The Tree of Life illustrates how different species arise from previous species via descent, with modification, and that all of life is connected. We share a common ancestor with all primates, but we are also fish, in the sense that fish are the most recent common ancestors of all land animals. If you keep building back from this idea, eventually you reach the single common ancestor or last universal common ancestor (LUCA).

Just about all evidence that researchers have been able to gather until now suggests that this universal common ancestor existed at some point between 3.5 and 3.8 billion years ago. Most scientists agree that it's a vastly more likely scenario that all life descended from a single ancestor than from multiple ones.

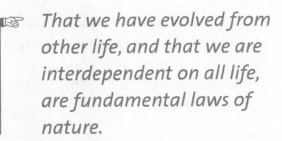 *That we have evolved from other life, and that we are interdependent on all life, are fundamental laws of nature.*

All forms of life survive by a mutual cooperation based on an innate recognition of their interconnectedness and often subtle interdependence. We are all part of – not apart from – everything, and many philosophers and spiritualists have long been aware that the universe is a unified whole where all things are part of a single system.

> *Human mind has not woven the web of life. We are but one thread within it. Whatever we do for the web, we do to ourselves. All things are bound together. All things connect.*

Chief Seattle

We are part of the *unity of all being*. Everything depends on something else for its existence and therefore all existence is relational. Life is connected because it comes from the same LUCA and information with function is passed on and modified over time. It is all one force with each bit interacting with other bits. The Tree of Life, although made up of many branches, is still only one tree.

Everything is a self-supporting ecosystem and is part of something bigger. We can only try to analyse the concepts of bigger and bigger and smaller and smaller within the limitations of our human processing. Maybe there is no maximum big and no minimum small, or no beginning and no end, and these are just human ideas.

The cosmic web

Some people think that the universe is just a hodgepodge of various planets, stars and galaxies. But over the years, scientists have found evidence that the universe may not be random, and it is actually more organised and interconnected than we could have ever imagined.

Earth is part of a solar system, and our solar system is one of many planetary systems and stars that make up the Milky Way galaxy. The Milky Way galaxy, as well as thousands of other galaxies, such as the Andromeda galaxy, belong to a collection of galaxies, called the Local Galactic Group. The Local Galactic Group is part of the Virgo Supercluster of galaxies, which some scientists say is one of about 10 million such galactic superclusters. Struggling to understand the scale of this? Me too, but let's just say that's a lot of planets, solar systems, galaxies and superclusters and all of these superclusters and everything we think we know in the universe forms an immense *network*, called the cosmic web.

So, what do we know about these planets and this web? First, all planets are in constant motion and, like the human body, they all resonate, circulate heat, and move around a central sun. Like humans, the solar system produces energy, it circulates heat and moves around a galaxy. Just like you, the galaxy resonates, it circulates heat, and it moves around a central universal core. Every human being, each planet, every sun and star, and each galaxy travels at its own pace and on its own track. Everything in this vast universe is in its own little world, yet we are all connected moving together in a fine-tuned and very precise symphony.

☞ *The next time you feel isolated, or inferior or superior to any other form of life, think about this connection. Humans are but a small piece of a massive creation.*

Changes in the universe affect our galaxy. Changes in our galaxy effect our solar system. Changes in our solar system affect the Earth. And changes on our planet affect human beings.

There are some things that we just can't understand in our lifetime, but it does seem likely that if we rewind time, then we go back to a single something, whatever we choose to call it, and *everything is expanding* from that. We are all derived from the same source. We are all related to this source, and this source of all life is always in all of us, like a ray from the sun is always from the sun. We are interconnected in terms of our make-up and origin, and our present is connected with our past, and the future is connected to the present. We are also connected to all other forms of life. Everything in the universe is like a three-dimensional interconnection or giant ball of infinite, hard-to-comprehend connections.

EXERCISE 36
Building Awareness That Everything is Interconnected

Sit calmly. Close your eyes and take several deep breaths. Focus on your body, being aware of the different parts.

Start with your feet and work up, thinking about how the parts of your body are interconnected.

When you are ready, think about your life and how it is connected to your past. Where you are right now is because of all the events that happened before.

Think about the future and how what you do next links to everything in your future.

Next, think about other people and how you are connected, starting with those closest to you.

Think of all forms of life – animals and plants, and all of nature – as one big ecosystem with which you are interconnected and interdependent.

Think of this ecosystem as part of a bigger ecosystem, which in turn is part of something bigger.

> *Think of the universe and everything at the highest level you can. It is all interconnected.*

Interdependence

Nothing we ever do stops. Every act is a link in an endless chain that is connected with all the other links. And this chain of the universe, unites all objects and processes in a single whole. Even by moving our finger we 'disturb' the whole universe which is an infinite web of connections which interact either through various fields or by means of direct contact. In a crystal, for example, which is a mix of atoms, no individual atom can move in complete independence of the others. Its slightest shift has an effect on every other atom.

 If we become more aware of the interdependence of everything then our respect for every other living thing in the universe will change.

Realising we are all one, that we are all in this together and we are all on the same team will make us more sensitive to the consequences of all our actions and lead to a happier, more peaceful and loving life.

Thinking of being separate from other people, from other things and life forms in the universe, is at the heart of many of our problems. We must awaken from this illusion of separateness and become more aware of what Larry Dossey calls our 'expansive consciousness', embracing the whole of nature in a 'non-local mind'. Even though we may live our lives in our local minds and ordinary reality, we are unconscious participants in this larger non-local mind. By being *happy, loving and grateful*, you are giving the greatest gift you can to this larger consciousness and you are aligned with your purpose of enjoying life and helping others.

> *The idea that everything is purposeful really changes the way you live. To think that everything you do has a ripple effect. That every word that you speak, every action that you make affects other people and the planet.*

Victoria Moran

STEP 7
Raise Your Vibration

If you want to find the secrets of the universe, think in terms of energy, frequency and vibration.

Nikola Tesla

Everything in our universe is interconnected and moving, because of the force we call energy. Let's start with you. Try to sit absolutely still for a moment. When you're sitting as still as you think you possibly can, ask yourself: is anything moving? Whether you're aware of it or not, your body is always moving. It is a *system* of systems, of organs and cells, which are always active, growing, transforming and replenishing. Our bodies are always in a state of movement even if we think we're still, and our organs are processing 24/7, whether it be our heart, liver, kidneys or lungs. Even if you held your breath to try and briefly be still, your heart would be beating around 4,000 times an hour, without you having to do anything consciously.

You are always moving

You can never be absolutely still. The estimated 37 trillion cells that make up our bodies are always moving, changing, renewing, constantly communicating with each other and keeping our hearts beating, digesting our food, eliminating toxins, protecting us from infection and disease, and generally being very busy carrying out all the functions that are keeping us alive. Even on the outside of our body, on the surface of human skin, scientists believe there are over 150 species of bacteria, which are in constant motion. Our hair and nails are growing, we sweat, and we discharge processed waste in various ways. We get bigger or smaller, we are always in a state of change.

Our brain constantly whirs, with neurons firing and chemicals being released. Even if you try to quieten your mind and not really think of anything, electrical and chemical processes are still occurring. Thinking is the nature of your brain. It is always 'doing' thinking. Even if you slow the processes, you simply can't stop thinking. You can focus and channel your thoughts effectively, you can detach from the thoughts you have and become a witness and observer of them rather than reacting, but you can't stop the process of thinking. If you are meditating, being mindful or even sleeping, your brain is still very active.

Our bodies are movement, and movement is a key to keeping them healthy. We are born as moving creations, with energy flowing through what is a miraculous system.

Movement is life. Life is a process. Improve the quality of the process and you improve the quality of life itself.

Moshe Feldenkrais

Our body system is in a constant state of communication within itself and it has its own built-in intelligence that is always there whether we're aware of this or not. Your heart, which was being created before you had a brain, may be the core of your innate intelligence system. Scientists have been researching how the heart thinks for itself and communicates with the brain, or in many ways can be considered a brain itself. Perhaps all parts of your body think for themselves. We know everything in life is interconnected and everything is a system, and so *communication* within our body must be happening in this same interconnected way, whether we're aware of this or not.

EXERCISE 37

Appreciate the Processes That Are Your Body

Sit calmly and take several slow, deep breaths. With each inhale and exhale, think about the flow of air into your lungs, with fresh oxygen being distributed into your blood and to your cells, and these cells then disposing of their waste, which is exhaled by your lungs and pushed out through your mouth.

Become aware of just how much there is to the process of taking a single breath, and how there is continual movement with this simple act of breathing.

Next, think about your heart. Feel it beating. Imagine with each beat, the journey of your blood being pumped, which is giving life and nutrition to your cells, travelling along arteries and veins.

Now bring awareness to other parts of your body and imagine the processes when you blink, when you look at something, when you hear a sound.

Of course, you can do this exercise for any of your body processes, at any time and wherever you are. And by bringing occasional consciousness to what's going on inside, you will also be building your appreciation for the miraculous system that you are.

Waves of energy

Many things are moving, which are not visible to us and which we are unlikely to be aware of. We may be conscious of movement in the form of waves, such as sound, light and Wi-Fi, even if we don't really understand how they operate. Each wave is a wave of energy, but each has its own individual properties and is in some way different from every other wave. Life, it seems, is essentially differences and movement.

Soundwaves carry noises through the air to our ears. Seismic waves travel inside the Earth and cause earthquakes. Light, heat and radio energy are all carried by a variety of waves in the electromagnetic spectrum.

All existence can actually be explained by wave properties, and the flow and patterns of energy. We have *waves of energy* that are moving inside us constantly, including thought waves and the waves of emotion. All these waves, whatever type they are, have a structure and properties, such as frequency, period, amplitude, wavelength and speed.

We are slowed down sound and light waves, a walking bundle of frequencies tuned into the cosmos. We are souls dressed up in sacred biochemical garments and our bodies are the instruments through which our souls play their music.

Albert Einstein

Frequency is the number of wave cycles that are completed in one second, measured in hertz (Hz). A wave with a frequency of 20 Hz completes 20 wave cycles every second. If a frequency is vibrating fast enough, it's emitted as a sound, and if it vibrates faster, it's emitted as a colour of light. Each category of waves has a frequency spectrum. In the spectrum for visible light, violet is at the top with the highest frequency. At the bottom is red, which has the lowest frequency, and if waves have frequencies lower than red or higher than violet, it's not possible for humans to see them.

The amplitude of a wave is measured by its height and how much energy is being transported by the particular wave. The greater the amplitude (more height), the more energy a wave has, and the lower the amplitude (less height), the less energy is transported. Our thoughts and the emotional energy they cause to move in different ways around our bodies are waves in exactly the same way as other waves, and so they too have different frequency and amplitudes.

Your energy vibrates and this vibration produces waves flowing inside you, but these waves also flow out from you. You are a beacon, transmitting invisible waves of your energy out into the world. If your thoughts are negative you'll emit waves with low frequencies and amplitudes. If your thoughts are positive, you'll emit waves with high frequencies and amplitudes. By managing your mind more effectively (Step 2) and taking charge of your emotional energy (Step 3), you can focus on ensuring that your thought patterns are creating waves with high frequencies and amplitude, by positive happy empowered thinking. This will not only make you feel great because of your higher vibration, but you'll also be transmitting more positivity to others.

Your energy introduces you even before you speak.

Anonymous

Understanding your brainwaves

Scientists are understanding more about how energy flows, as machines for measuring electric impulses are becoming more sophisticated. It is now commonly accepted that neurons in our brains fire together in *rhythmic patterns* like a kind of clapping, and the frequency of these patterns is measured like all waves; in hertz or cycles per second. Slow clapping, or slow waves, therefore measure as low frequency, and fast clapping or fast waves measure as high frequency. Modern equipment for measuring brain electrics shows that there are five basic brainwave types in terms of frequency; delta, theta, alpha, beta and gamma. They all have a frequency range, and each wave type controls a variety of states of consciousness ranging from sleep to active thinking. While all brainwaves work simultaneously, one brainwave can be more dominant and active than others and the dominant brainwave will determine our current state of mind.

Delta brainwaves are slow, less than 4Hz. They tend to be generated in deepest meditation and dreamless sleep, and when delta brainwaves are dominant, external awareness is suspended. It is believed that healing and regeneration are stimulated in this state, and this is why deep restorative sleep is so essential to the healing process.

Theta brainwaves, with a frequency of around 4 to 8Hz, occur most often in REM (Rapid Eye Movement) sleep but they are also dominant in meditation and are believed to be a gateway to learning, memory and intuition.

Alpha brainwaves (8 to 12Hz) are dominant during quietly flowing thoughts and in some meditative states, being described by some as waves of being here in the present moment. Alpha is a resting state for the brain and it is believed these waves aid our overall calmness, alertness, learning and our mind/body integration.

Beta brainwaves (12 to 40Hz) dominate our normal waking state of consciousness when attention is directed towards cognitive tasks and the outside world. Beta is a 'fast' activity, present when we are alert, attentive, engaged in problem-solving, judgement, decision-making, or focused mental activity.

Gamma brainwaves (greater than 40Hz) are the highest frequency or fastest waves and they relate to simultaneous processing of information. They are associated with high levels of intellectual function, creativity, peak states or what we might call feeling 'in the zone'.

 Our brains activate and constantly transmit waves, but they also receive waves.

Thoughts, ideas, information and knowledge from the universe can be tapped into, depending on the habitual frequency of your own thoughts and emotions. It all starts with *energy and frequency*. Everything is interconnected, and you can be a better manager of what you transmit and receive when you understand and better manage your frequencies.

Beyond our senses

Think about the remote control for your TV. At the end of the unit, there's a small light-emitting diode (LED) where infrared radiation comes out, and on the TV is a very small infrared light detector. When you press a button, a beam of infrared radiation travels from the remote to your TV at the speed of light and the detector picks it up. Human eyes can't detect these infrared remote-control waves, but some animals can. We describe these waves as invisible, but they should more accurately be described as 'invisible to humans'. Understanding these limitations and that we can only experience life through a limited range of senses, might help us humbly appreciate that there is a lot more to the universe than we can likely ever know in this existence.

Think of the incredible sense of hearing that we have. Dolphins, bats and some shrews, however, have a much greater hearing capacity and they use echolocation to navigate their surroundings. They emit high-frequency soundwaves or pulses that are either very high-pitched to human ears or completely inaudible, and then detect the echoes produced by those sounds. Special ear and brain adaptations enable these animals to build three-dimensional pictures of their surroundings in the way doctors use echo-scanning tools for imaging tests like pregnancy and heart scans.

Many animals have a much stronger sense of smell than humans. Dogs, for example, have about 600,000 olfactory neurons in a specialised recess, which is about 15 times the amount humans have, and which is why dogs are great for use in drug sniffing and finding skiers in avalanches. Not only do dogs have powerful, super-sensitive smell capabilities, they have much more sensitive hearing than humans, hearing sounds four times farther away and picking up much higher frequency sounds than we can.

The movement of molten material in the Earth's core and the flow of ions in the Earth's atmosphere generate a magnetic field that surrounds the planet. Just as compasses point toward magnetic north, animals possessing a magnetic sense can orient themselves in specific directions and navigate long distances. Animals as diverse as bees, sharks, sea turtles, rays, migratory birds and salmon all have magnetic senses. Even the lowly worm relies on a single nerve that detects Earth's magnetic field and orients them accordingly, so they aren't upside down.

Bees use the hair on their legs to detect a flower's electromagnetic field, and although they rely on many variables to find roses in your garden, one of the most important is voltage. They accumulate a small positive charge as they fly, and flowers have a negative charge. The hairs on their legs respond to the attraction between these opposite charges, guiding them to flowers, and this charge changes once a bee stops, so other bees know to move along.

We share our planet with creatures that can smell veins, see colours we can't imagine, hear sounds we don't hear and who can communicate through their feet. All of this is because of energy, and energy moving in different waves. We know there are many types of these waves, but the key point is to be acutely aware that energy is causing movement everywhere and in everything. *Everything is energy.*

Our electromagnetic field

Scientists today have equipment which can test for the electric charges humans are transmitting. Our body is constantly processing and the electricity we are generating from all of our body workings, not just our brains, creates an electromagnetic field, which can actually be measured. We have a powerful overall *electromagnetic field*, extending about 15 feet from our physical bodies, and different parts of us have their own individual energy fields, such as the lungs, the brain and the heart, with all parts being in systems that are part of larger systems inside us.

The heart has an electromagnetic field believed to be 40 to 60 times stronger than the brain's, and there is an increasing amount of study looking at how important it is for our heart to be aligned electrically with our brain and all our body systems.

The leader in the field of research in this area is the HeartMath Institute. It has conducted extensive studies that show we will feel most at peace and content in our life when our heart energy is aligned with our brain energy in a state of coherence. The HeartMath Institute's understanding is that through an unseen electromagnetic energy emitted by the heart, humans are profoundly connected to all living things, and that it is the energy of our hearts that literally links us to each other. We are all part of and contribute to the collective energy field.

EXERCISE 38
Feel Your Electricity

Stand comfortably with your feet shoulder-width apart.

Put your arms out straight in front of you and rub the palms of your hands firmly together, back and forward quickly for 15 seconds.

Now bring your palms very close together, but not quite touching.

What can you feel? You will probably feel something if you did this correctly.

This is energy. You are electric!

Now put your arms out in front of you again, and hold your palms upwards. Focus on your palms.

What do you feel? Some sensations? Tingling?

You are energy. It flows through you and is all around you. Everything is energy.

You are an *energy communicator*, constantly transmitting energy, and what you contribute to your energetic field environment, like every action or movement, has consequences. The collective magnetic energy fields of all human beings across the world make up a global energy field and it may be that; the emotions you feel, whether positive or negative, the energy you create and your acts of kindness affect your field environment and affect all life, as all things are interconnected by connection to the Earth's magnetic fields.

Everything is in motion

Everything in the universe is always in motion and the universe is expanding. Humans are always moving. Other forms of life are always moving. Earth is always moving. All the planets are moving, galaxies are moving and the universe is always moving, and all the movement is because of energy.

Even though it may look as if you are just sitting still sometimes, you are actually not only moving a lot on the inside, but also at great speed externally on the Earth, which is moving around the sun, in the moving Milky Way, among other moving galaxies and through the expanding universe! All because of energy.

We know everything is moving but what about items in the universe that we think of as solid or still? What about rocks, or a chair? We know that the Earth on which these objects exist is moving, but quantum physics explains that at a subatomic level, these 'solid' objects are also moving.

Things that look solid are made up of *vibrational energy* fields at the quantum level and anything that exists in our universe, whether seen or unseen, broken down into and analysed in its purest and most basic form, consists of pure energy or light, which resonates and exists as a vibratory frequency or pattern. Solid matter, as we conventionally understand it, does not exist because all the particles that make it are merely vibrations of energy. A table may look solid and motionless but within the table are millions and millions of subatomic particles running around and bouncing with energy. At the atomic, subatomic and quantum levels, the table is pure energy that vibrates. Everything is energy and energy vibrates.

Nothing disappears, it just changes form

Where does this energy come from? Whatever you believe about the ultimate origins of energy, it may be helpful to accept that we just don't know for sure, and that this is the beautiful unknown of being alive.

The energy we encounter and use every day has always been with us since the beginning of the sun and the universe, it just changes form all around us by the law of the conservation of energy. Nothing ever disappears, it just changes form and the ideas of a beginning and an end are maybe human concepts that, in terms of energy, are unhelpful.

Everything in life is vibration.

Albert Einstein

We know that everything in our universe exists as a vibratory *frequency or pattern*. Everything is vibration. We are transmitters and receivers of energy and vibration, radiating our own unique energy signature. We are made of cells, which are made of atoms, which are made of particles, which are actually just vortices of energy, constantly spinning and vibrating uniquely, and our 'vibrational fitness' is important, not only to our own body, mind and spirit, but to everything in the universe.

Become more aware of your vibrations

Different parts of us have different vibrations, at different times, and this energy is always flowing and changing form. The higher the frequency of our energy or vibration, the lighter we will feel physically, emotionally and mentally. We will experience greater personal power and clarity.

When you become more aware of your vibrations and the flow of energy within and around you, you can consciously channel this and bring focus to creating the life you want.

We can control our vibrational frequency to attract to us that which matches our vibration.

It might all seem abstract and hard to comprehend if you're new to the concept of vibrational energy, but it is possible to see a physical expression of *invisible energy waves* or vibrations in a process called cymatics, which is effectively the science of how soundwaves affect matter. Sand is subjected to different sounds, or frequencies, and these vibrations create different geometric shapes in the sand because of the waves.

Every frequency that passes through our bodies and minds is organising the molecules of our bodies. Just like how our fingerprints are unique, so too the energy field of each person and your body, which is 70% water, is always responding to the vibrations around it.

> *Energy moves in waves. Waves move in patterns. Patterns move in rhythms. A human being is just that, energy, waves, patterns and rhythms. Nothing more. Nothing less. A dance.*

Gabrielle Roth

Your vibrations determine what you attract

Your 'vibration' is really just a fancy way of describing your overall state of being. You may have heard of the 'law of attraction', which describes the ability to attract into our lives whatever we are focusing on using the power of the mind to translate our thoughts into reality.

 If you focus on negativity you will remain in the pattern of sending and receiving negative vibrations.

If you *focus* on positive thoughts and have inspirational goals, you will find a way to achieve them. Everything that manifests in your life is there because it matches the vibrations from your thoughts. The energy of your thoughts creates your reality, so it's important to become acutely aware of your thoughts, words and feelings. The lower your vibration the more likely you are to attract circumstances that mirror this, and the higher the vibration, the more good you will attract. Like energy attracts like energy.

EXERCISE 39
Monitor Your Vibrations

Ask yourself at the end of any day: How have I been vibrating? How did my vibrations flow and change?

Draw a simple graph to show your vibrations throughout the day, scoring yourself on a scale of 1 to 10, where 10 is when you felt you were vibrating at a very high frequency and 1 for when you felt you were vibrating at a very low frequency. Draw a line across the bottom of a piece of paper, showing the time of day in hourly intervals, and then draw a line up from the start of that line showing your score scale of 1–10.

You can now plot how you think you were vibrating at different times of the day.

Let's call this your 'vibrational frequency graph' and, of course, it is not an exercise in trying to be exact, but rather to encourage you to become more aware of how you are vibrating.

The highest levels of vibrational frequency include love, appreciation, peace, joy, acceptance and courage, so practice being in these states.

By raising your vibration you will create a more fulfilling and connected life.

Change your inner thoughts to the higher frequencies of love, harmony, kindness, peace and joy and you'll attract more of the same.

Wayne Dyer

Build awareness of your vibrational frequency. The vibration of the thoughts you have will create the life you will have, so it's smart to raise your energy to its highest vibration to get a deeper and more fulfilling connection with the universe. You can practice raising your vibration in lots of ways, and the more you practise, the more you will unconsciously or *habitually* vibrate at higher frequencies.

EXERCISE 40
Practise Raising Your Vibration

There are many ways you can raise your vibrations and if you have been following the SYSO System you are likely already living at a higher frequency more often than you were in the past. However, here are just a small number of examples of actions you could take to elevate your vibrational energy. These will not only make you feel better but, you will also be more fun to be around.

1. *Move your body. The human body is made to move. Make sure you have scheduled lots of movement in your day in whatever form you enjoy. There are endless ways to move. You don't have to call it exercise, that's just a label, but find regular fun ways to keep physically active.*

2. *Sing. It doesn't matter how good you think your singing is, but singing is possibly one of the most underrated things you can do to raise your vibration. Singing releases endorphins and oxytocin, improves cognition, can lower blood pressure, tones your facial muscles, and can boost your immunity.*

3. *See people you love frequently and tell them how much they mean to you and how you appreciate them in your life.*

4. *Laugh! We know laughter is the best medicine. Laughing is an express vibration-raiser. Laughing feels good and it's contagious.*

5. *Volunteer and contribute.*

6. *Surround yourself with colours that uplift you.*

7. *Make your environment a happy place and clear of clutter.*

8. *Practise gratitude. Become more aware of all the things you love and how abundant you really are. Make notes of the things you are grateful for.*

9. *Foods have a vibrational energy, so eat healthily to nourish every cell in your body. Processed foods, sugar, bad fats and salt have a low vibrational energy.*

10. *Drink water. It is an energetic life force that cleanses and hydrates your body. We are made up of 70% water and we need to flush out toxins to keep our vibrational energy levels up.*

11. *Schedule quiet time to meditate and feel a sense of calm.*

Energy healing

The body used to be thought of as a three-dimensional anatomical structure, but recently there has been a far greater awareness that the body is actually a process, with a constant flow of *energy and information.*
Energy healers have known this for a long time, but many conventional medical practitioners have dismissed energy healing as scientifically unproven. There is, however, now a growing body of evidence about not just the mind/body connection in healing, but also on many of the specific practices that focus on how energy is flowing through our bodies.

> *In every culture and in every medical tradition before ours, healing was accomplished by moving energy.*

Albert Szent-Györgyi

For centuries, healers in several traditions have believed in the energetic body. In India, Japan, China, Thailand and Tibet there has long been a belief in channels of energy, or meridians, or *sens* or *nadis*, along which our vital life energy flows. Life in these traditions is considered to be a bioelectrical and vibrational energy phenomenon, and being healthy involves balancing energy.

Even though traditional medicine hasn't been open to these less measurable energy healing practices until recently, science has understood that our bodies are electromagnetic and has measured these frequencies using, for example, electrocardiographs (ECGS) and magnetic resonance imaging (MRI) for many years. Our bodies are an energy field and we are immersed in energy fields, from the Earth's magnetic field to the fields produced by our heart, organs and cells. Our bodies *are* energy. They have an electrical nature. You will probably have experienced an electric shock and if you cut yourself, you will feel the pain, because a message is carried along nerves electrically to your brain. *You are an energy being.*

EXERCISE 41

Channel Healing Energy

Find somewhere comfortable and quiet where you can stand without distraction.

Loosen your shoulders and body and stand with your feet comfortably apart. Inhale deeply for five seconds, followed by a long exhale of at least six seconds.

Do this four or five times, feeling the ground firmly supporting your feet and body.

Now imagine an invigorating force of powerful healing energy coming down from above into your head and through your body, before going out through your feet, and then carrying on down to the very core of the Earth.

Breathe deeply in a rhythm that feels comfortable, feeling your feet perfectly supported by the Earth beneath you, and then imagine this electricity or life force of pure energy running from the core of the Earth back up through you, healing every cell in your body, before passing back out through your head.

Do this quickly several times until you feel you have found a pace that you like.

See this refreshing energetic healing force moving into you, down through your body, out to the Earth's core, back into you, through you and out to the universe.

Focus on your breathing, focus on the healing energy moving through you, and feel grateful for this life force that is always available to you.

Tuning into the energies of the universe

Tuning into your inner life force and being receptive to the subtle energies of the universe is at the core of all energy practices.

 If energy work is new to you, keep an open mind and be aware that there is so much as humans we don't know.

There are many energy healing practices. Try some of the methods if you haven't experienced them before. Find a local practitioner if you need one and as a minimum, incorporate meditation and movement into your routine. Build awareness of energy flow and find practices that work for you.

One area of energy work that is increasingly being incorporated into mainstream well-being is breath work.

We have looked at this already in some of the exercises. Breath work just refers to any type of breathing exercises or techniques designed to improve energy flow and health. We know how important breathing is in exercise, meditation and yoga, where you intentionally change your breathing pattern to change how you feel, which works by oxygenating the body and increasing blood flow. Studies reveal that by changing the patterns of breathing it is possible to reduce stress, relieve symptoms of anxiety, improve physical health and endurance. Rapid and deep breathing leads us to release more carbon dioxide from the body than usual, causing the blood to become more alkaline and retain more oxygen.

Whether you practice formal breath work or not, building awareness of how you are breathing and understanding the *physiological* changes breathing differently can cause, is very important for personal development and self-management.

EXERCISE 42
Practise Box Breathing

Sit upright, with your feet flat on the floor.

Slowly and deeply inhale through your nose counting to four.

After four seconds of deep inhaling, your lungs have now filled with air. Hold this breath for another slow count of four.

Then exhale through your mouth for four more beats.

Finally hold your breath counting to four.

Repeat this process several times and become aware of being in control of your breathing and how changing how you breathe can change how you feel.

This practice of four deep breaths in, holding for four, exhaling for four and holding for four, has been called 'square', or 'box', breathing and it can be done discreetly anytime to calm your nervous system and bring focus.

Be the creator of your life experience

Start making habits that build awareness of the energy that is you, and that is everything, and the power of this energy when directed. Consciously directing energy and attention to a new future and *manifesting* the life you want, is limited only by your ability to imagine it. When you tune into this, synchronicities, coincidences and new opportunities will appear in your life and you will start to become more aware of what you have been doing. By seeing the world differently and knowing that you are not a passive recipient, you create your life reality moment by moment. The energy fields of your brain are literally creating reality.

> *The vibration of appreciation is the closest vibration that can be experienced by a human being to that of their non-physical core energy.*

Abraham Hicks

EXERCISE 43
Practise Energy Gratitude

Just pause for a moment.

Bring your focus again to feeling your heartbeat, and to its energy.

Then bring the focus to your breath, and all the energy running through you.

This is your life force and this is a gift you were given by something greater than you.

Life wanted you to be. You are loved and you are also a source of love.

Feel this energy, and feel the power of this love that created you.

Be grateful for this moment, this day and all of life, and commit to being useful, and having fun, aligning fully with your life purpose.

Practise this regularly. It doesn't take long and you can do it anywhere.

Make it a habit!

The first Step of the SYSO System is to become more aware. As you have travelled through the other six Steps in this book you will have continued to expand your level of self-awareness, harnessing more of your unlimited potential. When awareness is contracted, the flow of energy and information through your body, mind and soul is restricted.

You can get caught up in toxic thinking like regret, resentment and self-pity and it's easy to succumb to unhealthy habits, like a lack of physical activity and negative mental processing. However, when you expand your awareness, your energy flows freely, you feel more balanced, at ease and creative, and you view yourself and the world with more understanding and compassion. You will be open to new possibilities for growth, and you will have all the power you need to create an outstanding, joyful, passionate, fun and useful life.

You are the architect of your life. You decide on your experience and you can always choose how you want to feel. Everything you need is within you right here, right now. You have the power. All you need to do is realise it.

> *It is your road. Others may walk it with you, but no one can walk it for you.*
>
> *Rumi*

Summary and Next Steps

> Your life will be no better than the plans you make and the action you take. You are the architect and builder of your own life, fortune and destiny.
>
> Alfred A. Montapert

Congratulations!

If you have read this far, you will understand that sorting yourself out isn't that complicated, you just need to know what to do and how to do it, and then you need to do the doing.

If you have followed the seven steps of the SYSO System, you are:

- Step 1 : Building your awareness

- Step 2 : Being a great manager of your mind

- Step 3 : Taking charge of your emotions

- Step 4 : Meeting your human needs in healthy ways

- Step 5 : Thinking clearly about the purpose of your life

- Step 6 : Understanding that everything is interconnected

- Step 7 : Raising your vibrations to make your life more fun and to enhance the lives of others.

You have lightened up, and are leading with your heart, not your ego. You are being focused on feeling fulfilled by being useful and having fun. By following the seven steps you have changed the filter through which you experience life, and by changing the filter, everything looks different. You have a new perspective, clarity of purpose and excitement about the amazing adventure that is your life.

Like any learning, there will be moments of great progress and flow and other times when it may feel challenging. Improvement seldom happens in a straight line, but when you start to see how far you have evolved, and experience how differently you feel, you can be proud of your growth, grateful for the lessons so far and excited about the future.

You can go back to any or all of the seven steps at any time, and the exercises in this book give you plenty of opportunities to practise. Repetition really is the mother of all learning and the foundations will become more deeply embedded in your unconscious mind with more repetition. The practise never stops, the growing possibilities are limitless, and the rewards of becoming more and living a joyful and fulfilling life will benefit not just you, but the whole universe.

Your growth and happiness are gifts to all of us.

Wherever you are on your life journey, you now have the foundations to create the future you want and the next step is to make a clear action plan for specific areas of your life. You need to know clearly and precisely where you are now, where you want to go to, why you want to go there and then start heading in that direction.

Your journey is unique and only you can decide where you really want to go; you have to set your destination. When you have this clarity, you will live more effortlessly and intentionally, knowing exactly where you are going and why, which will make the journey a lot more fun.

EXERCISE 44
Four Planning Questions

Write down the following four questions and always keep these to hand as you create your action plan. They will help focus your thinking and give your plan structure and clarity.

- ● *Where are you?*

- ● *Where do you want to go?*

- ● *Why do you want to go there?*

- ● *How are you going to get there?*

These are the big simple overriding questions that should inform your action plan and we will now look at how to approach answering them.

1. Where are you? The first step is to take an audit of your current position. Directions to where you want to go depend on where you are starting from. So, start with an assessment of your life as it is right now. The clearer and more honest you are about where you are now, the more efficient your journey planning will be.

You can create a dashboard – like in a car – to bring focus to, and awareness of, the areas of your life that make up your overall experience. You can classify these in many different ways but these seven core areas are a good place to start:

- Body and vitality
- Emotions and meaning
- Time
- Relationships
- Finances
- Purpose
- Spirituality.

How are you doing in each of these areas? If you want to manage something, you have to be able to measure it, and if we want to measure it, we have to use numbers. So the next step is to think about each area of your life and assign it a number that represents how well you're currently doing.

EXERCISE 45
Create Your Life Dashboard

Draw seven large circles of approximately equal size across a piece of paper, in landscape format. Let's call this your life dashboard.

Label each circle with one of the seven different areas:

Body/vitality, emotions and meaning, time, relationships, finances, purpose, and spirituality.

Now, put a score between 1 and 10 in each circle for how you think you are currently doing in that particular area, where 1 is 'dire, it couldn't be much worse', and 10 is 'absolutely incredible, I'm crushing it'. Don't over-analyse, just write down the number which intuitively feels like an accurate assessment of where you are now in that area of your life.

Once you have done this for all seven areas, look across your dashboard and see which areas need the most attention. Usually lifting one of your weakest areas will elevate the others.

Creating and constantly assessing your performance on your life dashboard is one of the most important personal development tools you can use. Not only does it bring awareness and focus, but you'll feel great satisfaction when you look back as you grow.

Be truthful! The truth will set you free. Only real honesty with yourself is going to help you get to where you can. There's no point in scoring your body and vitality as an 8 when you know it's a 4. What's important is how you're going to improve in the areas you choose. It isn't where you have been that matters, but where you are going. Even if you score yourself a 9 in all areas, there is still unlimited scope for improvement as growing and developing never stops and like the universe, we always have the capacity to expand.

When you have completed your dashboard, you have the coordinates of where you are now, and you can use these to propel yourself forward. Don't think about anyone else's dashboard. The only comparison to make is against your previous self and your previous dashboard. Your dashboard is an invaluable tool, so keep it somewhere you can refer to it easily. You will be able to look back in the future, celebrate your progress and feel proud of how far you have come.

2. Where do you want to go? Most people don't really know where they are going and only have vague goals like, wanting to be happier and healthier, making more money, travelling somewhere and having better relationships, but vagueness like this is the thief of success. Clarity is your power and clarity precedes success. The clearer you are about exactly what you want, the more your brain will work out how to get there. We know from Step 2 that once you set clear goals, your unconscious mind then has a target to work towards and it works best when given direction. Make your goals clear, specific and measurable, and your unconscious mind will work in its best way possible. The classic acronym SMART is a useful guide: Specific, Measurable, Achievable, Relevant and Time Sensitive. SMART goals give you clarity and a deadline for achieving them.

Make goals in the specific areas from your dashboard, deciding precisely where you want to be and by what date, and ask yourself if the goals are congruent with your overall life purpose. Every goal should feed in some way into, and be aligned with, your purpose for being here.

3. Why do you want to go there? You may know clearly what you want, but you also need to know clearly why you want it. Your 'why' is your fuel. When things get tough, or you feel like giving up on any goal, your 'why' is the power that will drive you forward.

For each goal, you need to know clearly your reasons. If your goal is to make more money (being specific about how much and when), then ask: 'Why do I want more money?' It may seem obvious and you might answer with something like 'so I can do more', but keep asking why and make sure your answer leads in some way to feeding your overall purpose. The more clarity you have around your goals and how they fit with your life mission, the more likely you will be to achieve them. If you start with the end in mind, all your steps should take you in that direction.

EXERCISE 46
Know Your Why

Pick three of what you consider to be your most important goals. You should do this exercise for all your goals, but let's just focus on what you consider to be your top three initially.

On a piece of paper create three evenly spaced columns and in the left-hand column write the three goals you have selected. These can be from any areas of your dashboard.

In the middle column, write your reasons for wanting to achieve each of these goals. The process of writing will help focus your thinking on the real underlying 'whys' that drive what you do.

In the right-hand column, write down how each of these goals fits with your overall life purpose.

You may not be used to examining the reasons that lie behind your choice of goals, but making this approach a habit will help make sure your goals are not only aligned with your life purpose, but also that you have the best 'fuel' to drive you towards them.

You can now examine all your goals and refine what is really important to you.

Thinking about your reasons, or the 'why' behind everything you do, should help you live more efficiently and effectively, aligned with your biggest why: your life purpose, which is your guiding star.

4. How are going to get there? Now you know where you are and have a clear vision of where you want to be and why, you just need an action plan of what you are going to do to get there. For each of your goals, starting with the one that needs most attention, focus on the steps you will take to get there. Understanding and planning are good, but *action* is what will get you the life you want.

> ☞ *Taking action towards clearly defined goals is the key to your progress. The distance between anything you want and making it reality is action.*

The path to success is to take massive determined action.

Tony Robbins

Now you can look at the various areas of your life and create a clear action plan for each. If you aren't taking action and moving in the direction of your goals, you need to work out what's stopping you. There could be practical reasons that just need a revised plan, but often the blocks we have to creating the life we want are internal barriers we make inside ourselves. These could be our beliefs, conflicts in our values or because we haven't learnt how to think effectively and create action-activating thought patterns. The tools you need to eliminate most of these potential internal blocks are in Steps 2 and 3, and as you have developed your awareness, you'll be able to spot these blocks early and make sure you focus on action and follow through.

A big reason people stumble is they haven't got an effective thinking technique in place when it comes to the moment of deciding whether to take action or not. As well as having a clear strong 'why' for fuel, you also need to practice self-discipline and make it a habit not to negotiate with yourself.

Remember, your mind works for *you*. If your plan is to exercise today but you are questioning whether to go and do this, you need to check in on your self-discipline habits. You know it is smart to go, you know it will make you feel good and you know it is part of your plan. So, don't negotiate with yourself, don't engage in an internal debate, just focus on your why and what it will feel like to have exercised and then just go. The hardest part is getting out of the door. As Jim Rohn said, 'You either pay the price of discipline or the price of regret', and as soon as you decide and take action you will already be feeling good that you did.

Making smart habitual 'go' decisions at these important action junctions is one of the most important techniques for achieving your goals. The more you make clear, action-activating decisions like this, the better you will feel about yourself, which will make you want to make *more* action-activating decisions. You can't bullshit yourself. Impressing yourself is a key part of building self-confidence and success, and a great way to impress yourself is to take action when you know there was a choice not to.

As you create your own clear and focused personal action plan, to take your life and your fulfilment to a whole new level, it is useful to keep a checklist of the seven steps of the

SYSO System at hand. The steps don't go out of date, they are applicable all the way through your life and are a distillation of what many of the most fulfilled people have known for a long time; life isn't that complicated unless you choose it to be.

EXERCISE 47
The SYSO System Checklist

Keep to hand the seven steps or principles of the SYSO System. Write them down somewhere easily accessible: on paper or on your phone, a notice board at your desk or on your computer.

Regularly check in with yourself to see how you are doing by asking these seven questions at any time:

1. *Am I becoming more aware?*

2. *Am I managing my mind to work for me?*

3. *How well am I taking charge of my emotions?*

4. *Am I meeting my needs in healthy ways and am I clear about the priorities?*

5. *Do I know clearly the purpose of my life?*

6. *Do I appreciate the interconnectedness of life?*

7. *How am I raising my vibrations?*

> *The quality of your life is largely determined by the questions you ask, and by asking these questions regularly you will automatically embed the seven steps of the SYSO System into your unconscious operating system.*

If you have read this book and taken the action suggested, your life will already be very different to when you started. You are in the driving seat, you are taking responsibility for your experience and you understand the invaluable role you play.

Everything you need to create an amazing life is already within you and you don't need to wait for anyone to light your fire. You have your own matches and now you know how to use them. Realise your power. Light up. Enjoy your life and shine on those you meet on your journey.

> *Those who are happiest are those who do the most for others.*
>
> *Booker T. Washington*

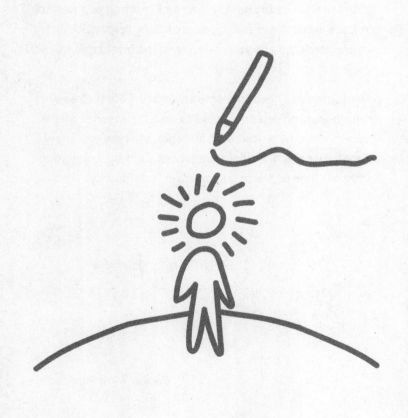

Notes and Thoughts

Realise Your Power

Realise Your Power

Realise Your Power